8.65

9/10/06

KIDS CAN COOK

By Dorothy R. Bates

Recipes Kitchen-Tested by Kids for Kids

D1486060

THE BOOK PUBLISHING COMPANY

SUMMERTOWN, TENNESSEE

Author
Dorothy R. Bates

Copy Editor & Layout
Kathryn Hill

Cover Art
Peter Hoyt

Color Photography
Stephen J. Owens

Black and White Photography
Nancy Fleckenstein
Russ Honicker

Line Drawings
Kathryn Hill
Albert K. Bates

Acknowledgements
Special thanks to all the kids in my cooking classes who cooked, ate and approved all the recipes and to my friends Virginia Daugherty, Bill Fern and Elizabeth Schoene who contributed recipes for us to try.

First Printing

ISBN 0-913990-58-2
Library of Congress Card Catalog
87-27664

TABLE OF CONTENTS

Secrets of Successful Cooks • 5

Useful Tools • 6

Ingredients • 7

Quick Breads • 9

Yeast Breads • 23

Soups • 33

Main Dishes • 43

Salads & Dressings • 71

Desserts • 83

Party Food and Menu • 107

Setting The Table • 116

Index • 117

Easy Recipes are marked with a ☆

INTRODUCTION

Kids like to cook if given a chance. For several years I've had cooking classes in my kitchen for kids from The Farm School, an alternative school in Summertown, Tennessee. Boys and girls ranged in age from 11 to 16. This book is a collection of recipes they especially enjoyed. They cooked for three hours, then we ate the three-course meal they'd prepared from start to finish.

They found that cooking can be fun and the reward is in good eating. They know that all it takes to cook successfully is to follow directions step by step. Their skill levels increased week by week and they found trying new dishes an adventure. Over the years, their requests and suggestions ("Can we try my grandma's Kolachy?") have enriched my own recipe collection.

Their genuine joy in cooking and their enthusiasm inspired this book. They chose the recipes and tested them all. They set a pretty table for our meals and washed the dishes afterwards. I appreciate the many happy hours we spent together and dedicate this books to kids everywhere who like to eat and will enjoy cooking.

Dorothy R. Bates

SECRETS OF SUCCESSFUL COOKS

Cooking is like riding a bicycle, the more you do it the better you get. Just remember:

1. Always read the recipe all the way through **first.**
2. Get out all the ingredients, these are in **bold face.** As soon as you have used the baking powder, baking soda, salt or spices <u>put that container away</u> so you don't use it twice.
3. Set out the tools and pans you will need. After you use one, put it in the sink to keep work area neat.
4. Wash your hands before you start. An apron will protect your clothes from stains. Tie back long hair so it doesn't get in your way.
5. Wash tools and clean your countertop as you go along to make final clean-up easy.
6. Ask for help with heavy or hot pans or pots. If you are not sure how to do something, ask someone.

For your safety:

1. Turn pan handles toward the back of the stove so the pan can't get bumped off.
2. Always use pot holders or oven mitts to lift lids off pans or remove food from the oven. Check position of oven racks before you turn on the oven.
3. Handle knives, peeler and grater carefully -- watch your fingers!
4. Treat machines with respect. Ask someone to show you how to work them. Don't put your hand into a food processor or blender, those blades are sharp!

USEFUL TOOLS

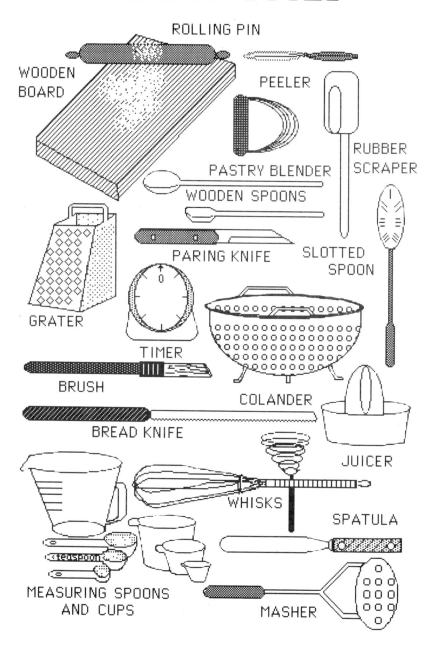

ROLLING PIN

WOODEN
BOARD

PEELER

RUBBER
SCRAPER

PASTRY BLENDER

WOODEN SPOONS

PARING KNIFE

SLOTTED
SPOON

GRATER

TIMER

BRUSH

COLANDER

BREAD KNIFE

JUICER

WHISKS

SPATULA

MEASURING SPOONS
AND CUPS

MASHER

Ingredients:

Ingredients are listed in **bold face type** in the recipes. Make sure you read the whole recipe and have everything you need before you start.

Measuring: Use level measurements, scooping up dry ingredient to overflow the cup or spoon, then leveling it off with the back of a knife. When measuring honey or other sticky ingredients, it helps to grease the cup first. To measure brown sugar, pack it into a measuring cup. Use a clean cup for dry ingredients.

Flour: We used unbleached all-purpose flour. Some prefer whole wheat or whole wheat pastry flour. You can substitute what you have and experiment.

Softened butter or margarine: Soften by slicing thinly onto a plate or hold wrapped stick in your hands.

Tofu: Some brands are softer, some firmer. It can be frozen in the package and darkens in color. Thaw frozen tofu before using and squeeze out all excess liquid.

TVP (Texturized Vegetable Protein), **Tempeh** and **Miso** are all soybean products available in health food stores. All are good sources of protein, vitamins and minerals, low in calories and are cholesterol-free.

Nutritional Yeast: Use only good tasting nutritional yeast, *(saccharomyces cerevisiae)*, grown on a molasses base. It comes in yellow flakes, has a cheesy flavor and supplies protein and B-vitamins.

Chris sifts flour before measuring.

QUICK BREADS

Breads of all kinds are fun to make and it's not difficult to make hot breads. These rise because of the baking powder or soda in the recipe and go with any meal.

☆Pancakes • 10
☆Apple Pancakes • 10
☆Blueberry Pancakes • 10
Waffles • 11
Pecan Waffles • 11
☆Honey Topping • 11
☆French Toast • 12
Baking Powder Biscuits • 12
Cinnamon Rolls • 13
☆Drop Biscuits • 14
☆Drop Cheese Biscuits • 14
Muffins • 15
Blueberry Muffins • 15
Date Muffins • 16
☆Raisin Bran Muffins • 16
Cornbread in a Skillet • 17
Coffee Cake • 18
Blueberry Coffee Cake • 18
☆Nut Bread • 19
☆Orange Bread • 19
Date Nut Bread • 20
☆Peanut Butter Bread • 21

Easy recipes are marked with a ☆

☆PANCAKES   about 12

You can tell the griddle is ready if a few drops of water sprinkled on it bounce. Some griddles need oil. Always make a test pancake first to check on the heat.

1. Heat a heavy griddle on medium high heat.
2. Measure into a quart-size bowl:

   2 cups flour
   1 tablespoon baking powder
   1 egg
   1 tablespoon honey
   2 tablespoons oil
   2 cups milk

   Stir together. It will be lumpy.
3. Use a one-third cup measure to scoop out batter for the test cake. Pancake is ready to turn over when bubbles appear on top. If it browns too fast, lower heat. Continue until batter is used up. Cover pancakes with a clean dish towel to keep warm.

☆APPLE PANCAKES

1. Make the batter for:
   Pancakes
2. Peel, grate and stir into the pancake batter:
   1 large apple

☆BLUEBERRY PANCAKES

1. Make the batter for:
   Pancakes
2. Wash, drain well and stir into the pancake batter:
   1 cup blueberries or blackberries

☆ WAFFLES   about 6

Read the directions for the waffle iron you use. Most have indicator lights that turn off when the iron is hot enough to pour in the batter. Oil the iron if needed. Waffle is done when iron stops steaming, don't open the lid to peek while it is cooking.

1. Sift into a medium size bowl:
   2 cups flour
   1 tablespoon baking powder
   1/2 teaspoon salt
2. In a small bowl, beat together with a whisk:
   2 eggs
   1/4 cup oil
   1 tablespoon honey
   1 1/2 cups milk
3. Stir liquids into flour mixture, but don't overmix.
4. Use a cup to pour batter onto the heated waffle iron. Make a test waffle first, then you will know how much batter to use. Bake until no steam comes out, waffle should be brown.

Note: *For fluffier waffles, separate the eggs, mixing the yolks in with the liquids; beat the whites to form soft peaks, fold beaten whites into the batter last.*

Pecan Waffles:

Add to the batter before baking:
   1/2 to 1 cup chopped pecans

☆HONEY TOPPING

1. Cream together until fluffy:
   1/2 stick butter or margarine
   1/4 cup honey
2. Put a spoonful on top of each waffle.

☆FRENCH TOAST   4 slices

1. Stir in a shallow bowl to mix well:
    1 egg
    1/4 cup milk
    1/2 teaspoon honey
2. Have ready to dip into the mixture:
    4 slices "day old" bread
3. Heat in a frying pan over medium high heat:
    1 tablespoon oil or margarine
4. Dip each slice of bread into the egg mix, coating both sides. Fry in the hot fat until golden brown. Do   one or two slices at a time. Add a little oil if needed.

BAKING POWDER BISCUITS   about 15

1. Heat the oven to 425°. Lightly oil a baking sheet.
2. Sift together into a bowl:
    2 cups flour
    1 tablespoon baking powder
    1/2 teaspoon salt
3. Measure out and add to the flour mix:
    1/3 cup vegetable shortening
4. Using a pastry blender, cut the shortening into the flour mixture until it looks like small crumbs.
5. Stir in with a fork:
    2/3 cup milk
6. Lightly flour a rolling pin and board.
7. With some flour on your hands, pat the dough out and roll it to about one-half inch thick, using a light stroke. Cut out biscuits, using a 2-inch cookie cutter or an empty tin can.   Push the scraps together into a ball and roll out for more biscuits.
8. Put biscuits on oiled baking sheet.
9. Put in hot oven and set the timer for 12 minutes. Peek at them, and if not lightly browned on top, bake a few minutes more. Remove to a board and serve warm.

CINNAMON ROLLS 12 rolls

1. Heat oven to 400°. Oil a 9" x 9" pan.
2. Make biscuit dough following directions on page 12. Gently roll the dough out into a rectangle that is about 12 inches long and 7 inches wide.
3. Mix together in a small bowl:
   2 tablespoons butter or margarine
   1/2 cup brown sugar
4. Sprinkle this mixture evenly over the dough, then roll up from the long edge so you have a long roll with the filling inside.
5. Cut the roll evenly into 12 slices.
6. Place slices in the greased pan. Bake in a hot oven about 12 to 15 minutes (set the timer), until lightly browned on top.
7. Use a pancake turner to remove hot rolls from pan.

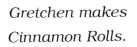
Gretchen makes
Cinnamon Rolls.

Erica puts Cheese Biscuits on a baking sheet.

☆DROP BISCUITS   about 18
These can be made fast, while the oven heats.
1. Follow directions for **Baking Powder Biscuits** on
   page 12, but increase the milk to use in all:
   > **1 cup milk plus 2 tablespoons**
   instead of 2/3 cup for rolled biscuits.
2. Dough should be soft enough to push off by the
   spoonful onto the lightly greased baking sheet.
3. Heat the oven to 425° before baking biscuits.
4. Bake the biscuits for 12 minutes (set the timer).

☆DROP CHEESE BISCUITS
1. Follow directions above (and on page 12) to make
   drop biscuit dough. After you add the milk for the
   soft dough, stir in **one of these:**
   > **1 cup grated jack cheese <u>or</u>**
   > **1/2 cup grated parmesan cheese**
2. If dough is too stiff to drop, add a little more milk. It
   should be a soft dough. Drop by the spoonful onto
   the oiled baking sheet and bake in the hot oven
   (425°) for 10 to 12 minutes. Set the timer.

MUFFINS

✗ not very sweet — try 4 T sugar

12 muffins

The secret of light muffins is not overmixing the batter. Try to combine the wet and dry ingredients in as few strokes as possible. Batter will be lumpy.

1. Coat 12 large muffin tins with margarine or butter. Or use baking cup liners in the pan. Heat the oven to 400°.
2. Sift together into a 2-quart bowl:
   - **2 cups flour**
   - **2 teaspoons baking powder**
   - ✗ **2 tablespoons sugar**
   - **1/2 teaspon salt**
3. Stir into flour mixture:
   - **1/4 cup dry milk powder**
4. With a large spoon, make a well in the center of the dry ingredients.
5. In a small bowl, whisk together:
   - **1 egg**
   - **1 cup water**
   - **1/4 cup oil**
6. Pour the wet ingredients into the well and combine wet and dry, stirring only 20 to 25 times with a large spoon. It's okay that it's lumpy.
7. Spoon the mixture into the greased muffin tins, filling each about two-thirds full.
8. Put in the hot oven and bake for 20 to 25 minutes, until lightly browned on top. (Set the timer).
9. Run a knife around the edge of each muffin tin to loosen muffin before lifting out to a serving plate.

BLUEBERRY MUFFINS

12 muffins

1. Pick over, rinse and dry on paper towels:
   - **1 cup blueberries**
2. Prepare muffin recipe above. Gently stir in berries after mixing the wet and dry ingredients. Be careful not to overmix. Continue with recipe. Blackberries are very good in muffins, too.

DATE MUFFINS   12 muffins

1. Prepare recipe on page 15 for
   Muffins, but:
2. Before adding liquids to dry ingredients, put into the
   flour mixture:
   1/2 cup chopped, pitted dates
   Stir the dates around in the flour to coat evenly.
   Then add the liquids and continue muffin recipe.

☆RAISIN BRAN MUFFINS   12 muffins

1. Heat oven to 400°. Grease 12 muffin tins with
   butter or margarine, or use baking cup liners.
2. Mix together in a medium- sized bowl:
   21/2 cups raisin bran cereal
   1 cup milk
   1/3 cup honey
   3 tablespoons oil
   1 egg
3. When these are mixed, sift into the bowl:
   1 1/4 cups flour
   1 tablespoon baking powder
4. Combine the bran mix with the flour mix is as few
   strokes as possible. It will be lumpy.
5. Spoon batter into muffin tins. Set the timer and
   bake for 20 minutes.

   Peek at them and if not lightly browned on top,
   bake a few minutes more. Oven temperatures vary.
   Remove from tins while warm.

CORNBREAD IN A SKILLET   8 servings

Baking this in a heated pan makes a crusty bottom.

1. Heat the oven to 375°.
2. Put into a heavy 10-inch black iron skillet:
     2 tablespoons oil
3. Put the pan in the oven to heat. Have potholders ready for lifting it out.
4. While oven and pan are heating, mix together in a medium-sized bowl:
     2 cups yellow cornmeal
     2 cups flour
     5 teaspoons baking powder
     1 teaspoon salt
5. Make a well in the center of the dry ingredients. Pour into the well:
     2 cups water or milk
     1/3 cup oil
     2 tablespoons honey
6. Use a big spoon to stir the wet and dry ingredients together, mixing them well.
7. Carefully lift the hot pan out of the oven, pour the cornbread batter into the pan, then set pan back in oven to bake.
8. Bake for 30 minutes (set the timer). It should be lightly browned on top and pulling away from the edges of the pan.

Note: This cornbread can be baked in a 9" x 13" pan instead of a skillet. Heat the pan with the oil before you pour in the batter.

COFFEE CAKE 9 squares

A very special breakfast treat you can make ahead.

1. Oil a 9" x 9" pan. Preheat oven to 375°.
2. Mix with a slotted spoon in a medium-sized bowl:
   1/2 stick margarine or butter
   1/3 cup honey
3. Beat together in a small bowl:
   1 egg
   1/2 cup milk
4. Stir the milk and egg into the butter and honey.
5. Stir in:
   2 cups flour
   2 teaspoons baking powder
   1/2 teaspoon salt
6. When batter is well mixed, spread it in the pan.
7. Then mix together in a small bowl:
   1/2 cup sugar
   1/2 cup flour
   1/2 teaspoon cinnamon
   1/2 stick margarine or butter, softened
8. Sprinkle this mixture evenly over the batter.
9. Bake for 45 minutes (set the timer). Cut into squares to serve.

BLUEBERRY COFFEE CAKE 9 squares

1. Follow the directions above for:
   Coffee Cake
2. After you mix in the flour, carefully stir in:
   2 cups blueberries
3. Then put batter in pan and sprinkle on topping. Bake the same as above.

☆NUT BREAD   1 loaf

Simple to make and simply delicious.

1. Grease a 9" x5" loaf pan. Heat oven to 375°.
2. In a medium-sized bowl, cream together, using a slotted spoon:
   1/2 stick margarine or butter
   1/3 cup honey
3. Stir in:
   1 egg
   3/4 cup milk
4. Sift onto a piece of waxed paper:
   2 cups flour
   2 teaspoons baking powder
   1/2 teaspoon salt
   Add the flour mixture to the bowl and stir until the batter is well mixed and quite smooth.
5. Stir into the batter:
   1/2 cup chopped walnuts
6. Spoon the mixture into the greased loaf pan. Bake it for 40 minutes (set the timer).
7. Test for doneness by sticking a toothpick into the center of the loaf. It it comes out clean, bread is done. Remove the pan from the oven and let it cool for 10 minutes, then remove loaf from the pan.

☆ORANGE BREAD   1 loaf

Follow directions for making **Nut Bread** above, but add with the walnuts (or instead of the walnuts):
   1 tablespoon grated orange rind
Use only the smallest holes on the grater and grate only the colored part of the orange rind.

DATE NUT BREAD   1 loaf

This is delicious sliced thinly and spread with cream cheese. Or made into little sandwiches for a party.

1. Grease a 9" x 5" loaf pan. Heat oven to 325°.
2. Place in a two-quart saucepan:
   I 1/2 cups dates, pitted and cut up
   3/4 cup hot water
3. Cook these over medium heat, stirring, 5 minutes.
4. Remove pan from heat and stir in:
   3/4 cup chopped walnuts
   1/2 stick margarine or butter
   1/2 cup honey
5. Let this mixture cool. While it cools, sift together onto waxed paper:
   2 cups flour
   1 teaspoon baking soda
6. In a small bowl, beat with a whisk:
   1 egg
   1 teaspoon vanilla
7. Stir the egg into the cooled date-nut mixture, then stir in the sifted flour and baking soda.
8. Spoon batter into the greased pan. Bake in the hot oven for 1 hour and 10 minutes. (Set the timer for an hour and test.) Stick a toothpick in the center of the loaf. When it comes out clean, bread is done.
9. Remove from oven and cool for 5 minutes, then turn loaf out of pan. Cool completely before slicing. Use a very sharp knife to slice thinly. Wrap loaf well and keep it in the refrigerator.

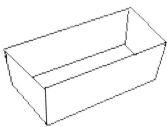

☆PEANUT BUTTER BREAD 1 loaf

If any bread is left over, it's very good toasted.

1. Grease a 9" x 5" loaf pan with butter or margarine. Heat the oven to 350°.
2. Measure into a bowl and set aside:
   2 cups flour
   2 teaspoons baking powder
3. Beat with a whisk in a two-quart bowl:
   1 egg
4. Add to the egg and stir well to mix:
   1/2 cup peanut butter
   1/4 cup honey
5. When it is well mixed, stir in the flour. Work it all together with a slotted spoon until no flour shows.
6. Stir in:
   3/4 cup milk
7. Stir until the milk is well mixed in. Then spoon it into the greased loaf pan.
8. Bake for 45 to 50 minutes (set the timer) in the oven. It will be lightly browned on top and pulling away from the sides of the pan when it is done.

Melina levels the flour for accurate measuring

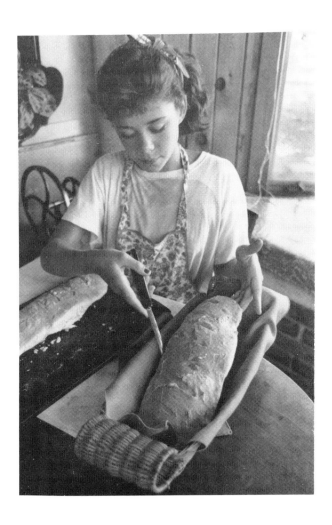

Gretchen puts Cuban Bread
in a basket for serving.

YEAST BREADS

Nothing smells better than bread or rolls baking in the oven and yeast doughs are fun to make.

You must be careful of the water temperature you use with yeast; water that is too hot or too cold will kill the action. Test it with your fingers to be sure it's hot, but not too hot for them. Honey, molasses or sugar added to the yeast will help the action. You'll find that flours vary in the amount of liquid they absorb. If the dough feels real sticky, add more flour. Be sure the oven is the correct temperature and set the timer.

☆Cuban Bread • 24

☆Hot Garlic Bread • 24

☆Oatmeal Bread • 25

☆Italian Rolls • 26

☆Poppy Seed Rolls • 27

Breadsticks • 27

Basic Fancy Roll Dough • 28

Cloverleaf Rolls • 28

Honey Buns • 29

Butter horns • 29

☆ Burger Buns • 30

Kolacky • 31

Easy recipes are marked with a ☆

☆CUBAN BREAD   2 loaves

This is an easy bread for beginners to make.

1. Into a large bowl, measure:
   1 tablespoon dry yeast
   1 tablespoon honey
   2 cups warm water
   1 tablespoon oil
2. Stir yeast mix, then add, one cup at a time:
   6 or 7 cups of sifted flour
   Flours vary in the amout of liquid they will absorb, add enough so dough isn't sticky.
3. Spread a little oil on top of the dough, then cover the bowl with a towel and let it rise until doubled in size. Punch down dough and divide it in half.
4. Prepare a baking sheet by sprinkling it with cornmeal. Or lightly oil the pan instead.
5. Shape the dough into two long loaves and place them on the baking sheet. Using a sharp knife, cut a few slashes in the top of each loaf. Let them rise 10 minutes. (Set the timer.)
6. Put a 9" x 13" baking pan of hot water on the bottom shelf of the oven. Then set the loaves on the shelf above it. Close the oven door, turn the oven on to 400° and bake the bread for 45 minutes. (Set the timer). This bread is best served warm. It makes good Garlic Bread.

☆HOT GARLIC BREAD   1 loaf

1. Heat the oven to 375°.
2. Cut in half lengthwise:
   1 loaf Cuban Bread
3. Mash together:
   1 stick margarine or butter
   3 sliced garlic cloves
4. Spread on halves of loaf. Cut into 2-inch slices.
5. Bake in the hot oven for 15 minutes. (Set the timer.)

☆OATMEAL BREAD   2 loaves

Very easy to make, this bread takes no kneading.

1. Measure into a big bowl:
   1 cup rolled oats (oatmeal)
2. Pour over these:
   2 cups boiling water
3. In a small bowl, put:
   1 tablespoon dry yeast
   1/3 cup warm water
   1 tablespoon molasses
4. Add to the oatmeal in the big bowl:
   2 tablespoons oil
   1/2 cup molasses
5. Stir this mixture with a big wooden spoon, then add the yeast mix. Slowly stir in:
   6 cups of flour
   1 teaspoon salt
6. When well mixed, cover the bowl and put in a warm place to rise until it is double in size.
7. Grease two loaf pans.
8. Press down the dough, divide in half and put into the pans. Lay a towel over the tops of the pans and let bread rise again. When it is almost double in size, heat the oven to 325°.
9. Bake the loaves about 55 minutes. (Set the timer.)
10. Remove pans from oven to a bread board and let cool for 10 minutes before you take the loaves out of the pans.

☆ITALIAN ROLLS   16 rolls

1. Put in a large bowl:
   1 tablespoon dry yeast
   1/4 cup warm water
   1 tablespoon honey
2. Let the yeast dissolve, then stir in:
   2 tablespoons oil
   1 cup warm water
3. Stir in:
   1 teaspoon salt
   4 cups of flour
4. Mix well together, dough may be stiff and hard to stir. If dough is sticky, add a little more flour.
5. Pat a little oil on top of the dough, cover the bowl with a towel and let it rise in a warm place until it is double in size. This takes about one hour.
6. Oil a baking sheet. With oil on your fingers, press down the dough and divide it into 4 smaller balls. From each ball, shape 4 round rolls and put them on the baking sheet. With your fingertip, lightly oil the tops of the rolls. Let them rise for 10 minutes while the oven is heating.
7. Heat the oven to 400°. When the oven is hot, bake the rolls for about 30 minutes until they are lightly browned on top.

POPPYSEED ROLLS   16 rolls

1. Prepare up to step #6:
   Italian Rolls
2. Place in a saucer:
   2 tablespoons poppy seeds
   As you shape each roll, dip the top into the seeds. You can also use either:
   2 tablespoons caraway seeds
   or:
   2 tablespoons sesame seeds
3. Continue with recipe.

BREADSTICKS   20 sticks

1. Prepare up to step #5:
   Italian Rolls
   Pinch off small balls of dough and roll it between your hands into sticks about 6 inches long and 1/2 inch thick. Place sticks on an oiled baking sheet.
2. Oil the tops of the rolls and sprinkle with your choice of seeds. Let rise 10 minutes while the oven heats.
3. Bake at 400° for 10 minutes only, then reduce the heat to 350° and bake for 10 minutes more. Be sure to set the timer so sticks don't burn. Sticks are delicious with caraway or sesame seeds on top.

BASIC FANCY ROLL DOUGH   24 rolls

This is the kids' absolute favorite to make and shape.

1. In a large bowl, dissolve:
    1 tablespoon yeast
    1/2 cup warm water
    1/3 cup sugar
2. Stir this and add:
    1/2 cup oil
    1 egg
    1 cup flour
3. Mix this sponge well, then add:
    3/4 cup water
4. Stir well, then stir in one cup at a time:
    4 cups flour
    Dough should be soft but not sticky. Add a little more flour if it feels sticky.
5. Oil the top of the dough, cover the bowl and let it rise for about an hour until double in size.
6. When it has risen, punch down the dough and make one of the following recipes.

CLOVERLEAF ROLLS   24 rolls

1. Prepare:
    Basic Fancy Roll Dough
2. Grease 24 muffin tins with butter or margarine.
3. Press down the risen dough. Melt:
    1/2 stick butter or margarine
5. With buttery fingers, pinch off small balls of dough and dip each in melted butter. Put three balls in each muffin cup, buttery side up. Cup should be two-thirds full.
6. Let rise until double, about one hour. Heat oven to 400°.
7. Bake the rolls for 20 minutes (set the timer).

HONEY BUNS   24 buns

1. Prepare up to step 2:
   Cloverleaf Rolls
   After you grease the muffin tins, put :
   1 teaspoon honey
   on the bottom of each tin. You can add **pecans.**
2. Continue with the recipe.
3. When rolls are baked, set them upside down on the serving plate.

BUTTERHORN ROLLS   24 rolls

1. Prepare:
   Basic Fancy Roll Dough
   Grease two cookie sheets.
2. When the dough has risen double, press it down and turn it out on a floured board.
3. Knead it 20 times, then divide in half.
4. Roll each half out into a circle with the rolling pin.
5. Put a little softened margarine or butter on the dough.
6. Cut each circle into 12 wedge-shaped pieces. Pull out the end of each wedge at the broad end and roll up toward the point. Place on a greased cookie sheet with the point underneath to prevent unrolling.
7. Brush the tops of the rolls with
   margarine or butter, melted
   and let rise about one hour until very light.
8. Heat oven to 400° and bake for about 15 minutes.

☆BURGER BUNS   12 buns

1. Heat in a l-quart pan almost to a boil:
   1 1/2 cups milk
2. Remove from heat and pour milk into a bowl. Add:
   1/4 cup oil or margarine or butter
   1/4 cup honey
   1 teaspoon salt
3. Let this cool down a little. Into a big bowl, put:
   1 tablespoons dry yeast
   1 teaspoon honey or sugar
   1/2 cup of very warm water
4. Stir to dissolve the yeast then stir in:
   1 cup flour
5. Beat this mixture 100 times, then let it rest for 5 minutes.
6. Add the milk and honey mixture, stir and add :
   2 cups whole wheat flour
   2 cups all purpose white flour
7. Mix dough well. If it's sticky, add more flour. When you can work the dough with your hands, put it on a floured surface and knead 10 times.
8. Oil a clean bowl, put the dough in it and turn it around to oil the top of the dough. Cover the bowl with a towel and let it rise for one hour.
9. Punch the dough down and divide it into 4 smaller balls. From each of these, shape 3 round buns.
10. Oil a baking sheet and set rolls on it. Let rise for 30 minutes. (Set the timer.)
11. Heat the oven to 375°.
12. When the oven is hot, put the rolls in and set the timer for 20 minutes. They should be lightly browned on top. Remove to a board and brush a little margarine or butter on the top of each roll. These are great for burgers or barbequed tofu.

KOLACKY *pronounced KoLATCHkee*   24 rolls

1. Mix in a small bowl:
     1 tablespoon yeast
     1 teaspoon honey
     1/4 cup warm water
2. Cream together with a slotted spoon:
     1 stick   margarine or butter, softened
     2 tablespoons honey
     1 teaspoon salt
3. Stir in and beat well:
     1 egg
     1 cup warm water
     1 cup flour
4. Add the yeast mixture and stir well together.
5. Slowly add, while stirring:
     3 to 4 cups flour
   Use enough to make dough soft but not sticky.
6. Turn it out onto a floured surface and knead it a few times. Put it in an oiled bowl and turn it around to coat with oil.
7. Cover bowl with a clean towel. Let rise for about 45 minutes, until doubled in size.
8. Knead down, pinch off balls the size of a walnut, place on a lightly greased baking sheet.
9. Let rise another 30 minutes. (Set the timer.)
10. Heat the oven to 400°.   Press down the centers with your thumb to make a small hollow. Fill each hollow with:
     1 teaspoon apricot preserves, <u>or</u>
     1 teaspoon peach preserves, <u>or</u>
     1 teaspoon apple butter
11. When oven is hot, put rolls in oven and bake for 12 to 15 minutes. (Set the timer.) Tops should be lightly browned.
12. Remove from oven and cool. If desired, sprinkle with:
     powdered sugar

Vivian cuts parsley to garnish Potato Soup.

SOUPS

Good soup fills up hungry people and homemade soups are the most satisfying. They are easy to make, can be made ahead, and any leftovers are good the next day.

☆Potato Soup • 34

☆Lentil Soup • 35

☆Vegetable Soup • 36

☆Alphabet Soup • 36

☆Miso Soup with Tofu • 37

☆Rice and Tomato Soup • 38

☆Corn Chowder • 38

Black Bean Soup • 39

☆Pea and Barley Soup • 40

☆Croutons • 40

☆Minestrone • 41

Easy recipes are marked with a ☆

☆**POTATO SOUP**   6 servings

1. Heat in a large pan on medium heat:
   6 cups water
2. Prepare and add:
   6 potatoes, peeled and quartered
   1 large onion, peeled and chopped
3. Cover the pan and bring to a boil over high heat. Reduce the heat to low and cook about 20 to 30 minutes, until potatoes are fork-tender.
4. With a potato masher, mash the potatoes up into bite-size chunks.
5. Add to the pan:
   1/2 teaspoon salt
   1 cup milk
   1/4 stick margarine or butter
6. Let this heat slowly (but don't let it boil). Ladle the hot soup into bowls and sprinkle on top:
   1/4 cup fresh parsley, chopped fine

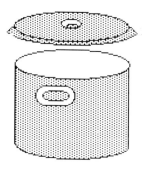

☆LENTIL SOUP   6 servings

1.   Rinse well and drain in a colander:
     1 pound dry lentils
2.   Place in a large pan with:
     8 cups water
     1 bay leaf
3.   Cover the pan and bring to a boil over high heat.
     Reduce the heat to low and cook the lentils for 30
     minutes.
4.   Meanwhile, cut into small pieces:
     2 cloves garlic
     1 large onion
     2 celery stalks
5.   Heat in a frying pan over medium low heat:
     1/4 cup oil
6.   Cook the onions and garlic in the oil for 10
     minutes, add the celery, cook 5 minutes more.
7.   Add the onions and celery to the soup pan. Add:
     1/4 cup tomato sauce or catsup
     1 teaspoon salt
     1/4 teaspoon pepper
8.   Cover the pan and cook over medium heat about
     20 minutes more, stirring once in a while. Taste
     for seasoning. Remove the bay leaf.

☆VEGETABLE SOUP   8 servings

1. Prepare by slicing or chopping 2 quarts of fresh vegetables, such as:
   1 large onion, peeled
   1/2 head cabbage
   3 carrots
   4 stalks celery
2. Heat a large heavy kettle over low heat. Put in:
   1/4 cup oil
3. Add onions, stir and cook a few minutes, then add cabbage. Cook and stir these 10 minutes.
4. Add carrots and celery and cook 10 minutes.
5. Add :
   2   quarts warm water
   1   teaspoon salt
   2   vegetable bouillion cubes
   (or use 2 teaspoons powdered
   vegetable bouillion)
6. Bring to a boil, cover pan, lower heat, cook about 20 minutes.

☆ALPHABET SOUP   8   servings

1. Prepare:
   Vegetable Soup
2. After simmering soup 10 minutes, add:
   1/2 cup alphabet noodles
   Cook 15 minutes more, until noodles are tender.

MISO SOUP WITH TOFU 8 servings

Miso tastes a lot like soy sauce, only it's a solid paste. It makes soups, sauces, gravies and casseroles taste good but it can be salty so add a little at a time.

1. Prepare:
   Vegetable Soup (page 36)
2. Dissolve by stirring together:
   2 tablespoons miso
   1/4 cup warm water
3. Stir the miso mixture into the soup. Don't boil the soup after adding the miso.
4. Cut into small cubes:
   1 pound tofu
   Place tofu in the soup to warm before you ladle the soup into bowls to serve.

Melina cuts napa cabbage for Vegetable Soup.

☆RICE AND TOMATO SOUP   6 servings

1. In a 2-quart pan over medium heat, melt:
   1/2 stick margarine or butter (1/4   cup)
2. Add and cook, stirring, for 5 minutes:
   1 cup raw rice
3. Prepare and add and cook until soft:
   1 medium onion, peeled and chopped
4. Add and stir in:
   2 cups fresh or canned tomatoes
   1 teaspoon salt
   4 cups warm water
5. Cover the pan and cook over medium heat until the rice is tender, about 40 minutes. This is a thick soup, you can add vegetable broth to thin it.

☆CORN CHOWDER   6 servings

1. Chop:
   2 small potatoes
   1 medium onion
   2 stalks celery
2. Heat in a 2-quart pan:
   2 tablespoons vegetable oil
3. Cook vegetables in oil for 5 minutes, then add:
   1 tablespoon powdered vegetable bouillion
   4 cups hot water
5. Cover the pan, reduce heat to low, cook for 20 minutes.
6. Add to the soup:
   2 cups fresh or frozen corn kernels
   1 cup milk
7. Cover and cook 10 minutes more on low heat.

BLACK BEAN SOUP   6 to 8 servings

This is so good, it can be a meal in itself, with warm Cuban Bread and a salad.

1. Wash and sort:
   1 pound black beans
2. Soak beans overnight in:
   3 quarts water
3. Drain the beans and add:
   3 quarts fresh water
   1 bay leaf
4. Bring the beans to a boil over high heat, then reduce heat to low, cover the pan and cook one to two hours until beans are tender. Take out a bean and squeeze it between your fingers to be sure they are done.
5. Chop up:
   1 large onion
   5 cloves garlic
   1 green pepper
6. Heat in a heavy skillet:
   1/4 cup oil
   Olive oil is nice to use. Fry the vegetables until soft. Add to the beans with:
   2 teaspoons cumin
   2 teaspoons oregano
   1 teaspoon salt
   2 tablespoons vinegar
7. Simmer together about 30 minutes.
8. Serve in bowls over a scoop of:
   cooked rice (page 52)
   and pass a dish of:
   red onions, chopped

☆PEA AND BARLEY SOUP   8 servings

This old-fashioned soup tastes wonderful on a cold or rainy day.

1. Rinse and drain:
   2 cups green or yellow dried split peas
2. Place them in a large heavy kettle with:
   1/3 cup raw pearl barley
   1 carrot, diced
   1 bay leaf
   8 cups water
   Bring to a boil, reduce heat to low, cover the pan and cook 30 minutes, stirring a few times.
3. Lightly fry until soft in a small pan:
   2 tablespoons oil
   1 onion, chopped
4. Add onion to soup with:
   1 teaspoon salt
   1/2 teaspoon garlic powder
   1/4 teaspoon black pepper
5. Cook another 25 to 30 minutes, tasting to see when barley and peas are tender. Check the seasonings.
6. Ladle into bowls. You can sprinkle on top:
   "bacon" bits or croutons

CROUTONS

1. Lightly toast, then cut in half-inch cubes:
   3 slices bread
2. Melt in a skillet, then fry cubes in:
   3 teaspoons margarine or butter
3. Stir them as they turn golden brown,
   then put on paper towel to drain.

☆MINESTRONE   6 servings

This is a good way to use up leftover beans or pasta or small amounts of any leftover cooked vegetables. This hearty soup makes a good meal served with salad and Italian bread or rolls.

1. Heat in a heavy 4-quart kettle:
   1/4 cup olive oil
   1 onion, peeled and chopped up
2. Cook this over low heat while you prepare:
   2 carrots, chopped
   2 stalks of celery, chopped
3. Add these and cook about 5 minutes, then add:
   3 cups water
   2 cups tomatoes, cut up
   1 teaspoon garlic powder
   1/2 teaspoon salt
4. Cook about 10 minutes, then add:
   2 cups cooked or canned beans
   2 cups cooked (leftover) pasta
5. Cover and cook about 20 minutes.
6. Ladle the soup into bowls and serve with a side dish of:
   parmesan cheese
   to sprinkle on top.

Ben tops Lasagne with cheese.

MAIN DISHES

Chili	•	44
Chili&Cornbread Topper	•	44
Pizza	•	45
☆Flour Tortillas	•	46
☆Bean Burritos	•	46
☆Beans from Scratch	•	47
☆Tofu Burritos	•	47
Enchilada Casserole	•	48
☆Easy Enchiladas	•	49
Chili Dogs	•	50
Pigs in a Blanket	•	51
☆Brown Rice	•	52
☆Rice with Herbs	•	52
☆Mexicali Rice	•	53
Chinese Fried Rice	•	53
Chinese Egg Rolls	•	54
Tofu Pot Pie	•	56
☆Noodle Casserole	•	58
☆Macaroni and Cheese	•	59
☆Lasagne	•	60
☆Italian Pasta Sauce	•	61
☆Mushroom Sauce	•	61
Stuffed Shells	•	62
☆World's Fair Specials	•	63
☆Easy "Sausage" Balls	•	64
☆Golden Gravy	•	65
Knishes	•	66
☆Kasha	•	67
☆Boofers	•	68
☆Nacho Pie	•	69

Easy recipes are marked with a ☆

☆CHILI   6 servings

1. Measure into a small bowl and stir:
   1 cup TVP (see page 7)
   7/8 cup very hot water
2. In a 2-quart heavy pan put:
   2 tablespoons oil
   1 medium onion, chopped small
   1 clove garlic, chopped small
3. Fry the onions and garlic over low heat until the onions are soft.
4. Add the TVP and fry 5 minutes.
5. Add to the pan:
   1 16-ounce can tomatoes (2 cups)
   2 cups water
   1 teaspoon cumin powder
   2 teaspoons chili powder
   1 teaspoon salt
6. Bring to a boil, cover, cook on low heat 20 minutes.
7. Break up tomatoes if they are big, then add:
   2 cups cooked pinto or red kidney beans (with liquid, if canned)
8. Cook for 20 minutes. Taste to check seasonings.

☆CHILI & CORNBREAD TOPPER

1. Heat the oven to 400°.
2. Pour into a 9" x 13" pan:
   1 recipe Chili (warm)
   (you can use canned chili)
3. Make according to directions on the package:
   1 pkg. (8 oz.) cornmeal muffin mix
4. Drop spoonfuls of dough on the chili.
5. Bake in the hot oven for 20 minutes until nicely browned on top.

PIZZA 4 10-inch pizzas

Crust:
1. Combine in a large bowl:
   2 teaspoons dry yeast
   1 teaspoon honey
   1 cup very warm water
2. Then stir in:
   3 to 4 cups flour
   1/4 cup oil
3. Knead the dough in the bowl a few times, then cover it and let rise for an hour. (Set the timer.)
4. Punch the dough down and divide into 4 equal-size balls. Cover them with a towel.
5. On a lightly floured surface, roll each ball out to a 10-inch circle with a floured rolling pin.
6. Lightly oil two cookie sheets and put two circles on each. Heat oven to 425°.

Sauce:
Mix in a small bowl:
   1 8-ounce can tomato paste
   1 teaspoon basil
   1 teaspoon oregano
   1 8-ounce can water

Assembly:
1. Spread the sauce evenly on the circles.
2. Sprinkle on toppings of your choice, like:
   1 large onion, sliced
   1 green pepper, sliced
   1/2 pound mushrooms, sliced
   Black or stuffed olives, sliced
3. Grate and put on top:
   8 ounces mozzarella cheese
4. Bake 15 to 20 minutes, until cheese is melted and crust is cooked. (Set the timer.)

☆FLOUR TORTILLAS   12 tortillas

1. Measure into bowl and stir with a wooden spoon:
   2 cups flour
   1/2 teaspoon salt
   1 cup water
2. Put a little oil on your hands and knead the dough a few times. Cover the bowl and let dough rest 15 minutes.
3. Lightly flour a rolling pin and wooden board. Make the dough into twelve small balls and flatten each out on the board. Roll into thin circles, turning the dough clockwise to keep it round.
4. When all the tortillas are rolled out, heat a skillet or pancake griddle on medium high heat.
5. When the griddle is hot, cook each one to barely brown, about 1 minute, and turn to cook the other side briefly. Brush one side with margarine or butter and stack them up until all are cooked. Keep covered with a towel to keep warm and soft.

☆BEAN BURRITOS   12 burritos

1. Have ready:
   3 cups cooked pinto beans
   1 red onion, chopped
   2 cups lettuce, chopped
   2 tomatoes, diced
   1 cup cheese, grated
   taco sauce, from a jar
   sour cream
2. Brown lightly on a greased griddle:
   12 flour tortillas
3. Put a big spoonful of beans on each one, let people help themselves to the toppings and roll their own.

☆BEANS FROM SCRATCH   6 cups

1. Put on a cookie sheet:
   2 cups dried pinto beans
   Sort out any stones and shriveled beans. Wash the beans well, rinsing in a colander.
2. Add:
   6 cups of water
   Soak several hours or overnight.
3. Drain the beans. Add fresh water to completely cover them, then add two cups more. Add:
   1 bay leaf
   to the beans, so they won't be gassy. Cover pan.
4. Bring to a boil over high heat, then reduce the heat to low, and cook slowly until tender.   This takes 1 to 2 hours. Add more water if needed.
5. Check a bean to see if they are done by squashing it between your fingers. Don't add salt until tender.

☆TOFU BURRITOS   12 burritos

1. You will need:
   12 flour burritos or tortillas
2. Mix together in a medium bowl:
   1 teaspoon flour
   2 teaspoons chili powder
   1 teaspoon cumin
   1 teaspoon salt
   1/2 teaspoon basil or oregano
   When spices are mixed, crumble in and mix:
   I pound tofu
3. Heat a heavy skillet on medium heat, add:
   3 tablespoons oil
   and the seasoned tofu mix.
4. Fry for about 5 minutes, using a pancake turner to keep it from sticking to the pan as it heats.
5. Put tofu mixture into tortillas, and prepare and serve accompaniments as for **Bean Burritos**.

ENCHILADA CASSEROLE　　8 servings

A big pan of enchiladas is always a hit and well worth the time it takes to make. Enchiladas are good with a tofu filling, too. Use the filling for Tofu Burritos.

You will need:

12 Flour Tortillas (page 46)
6 cups Chili Gravy (see below)
4 cups cooked pinto beans
2 cups grated cheese

Chili Gravy (6 cups):

1. Heat in a 3 or 4-quart kettle over low heat:
 1/3 cup vegetable oil
2. Chop and add:
 2 onions
 Fry until the onions are soft.
3. Measure out and sprinkle on top of the onions:
 2 tablespoons chili powder
 2 teaspoons cumin powder
 1 teaspoon garlic powder
 1 teaspoon salt
 1/4 teaspoon black pepper
 1/2 cup flour
 Stir flour and seasonings into the onions.
5. Slowly add to the kettle:
 6 cups warm water
 Keep stirring with a whisk to work out the lumps as you add the water. Cook this gravy over low heat for 20 to 30 minutes, whisking sometimes so it doesn't stick or get lumpy.

Assembly:
1. Heat the oven to 350°.
2. Pour into the bottom of a 9' x 14" pan:
   2 cups Chili Gravy
3. Heat a heavy skillet or griddle, oil it lightly, and cook the tortillas on each side about one minute.
4. Spread a big spoonful of beans down the middle of each tortilla, roll it up, set it in the gravy in the pan.
5. Continue to cook, fill and roll until all tortillas and beans are used.
6. Pour the remaining gravy over the enchiladas.
7. Top the casserole with:
   2 cups grated cheese
8. Bake for 40 minutes (set the timer).
9. Cut into squares to serve.

☆**EASY ENCHILADAS**   6 servings
This takes very little time to put together and is a good recipe for beginners or if you are in a hurry.

1. You will need:
   12 corn tortillas (1 10-oz. pkg.)
   1 10-ounce can enchilada sauce
   4 cups (2 cans) cooked pinto beans
   2 cups grated cheese
2. Heat oven to 350°, and oil a 9" x 14" pan.
3. Spread half the sauce on bottom of pan.
4. Place 6 tortillas on sauce, overlapping.
5. Spread the beans evenly on the tortillas.
6. Place remaining tortillas on top.
7. Evenly add the rest of the sauce.
8. Top with the grated cheese.
9. Bake for 40 minutes (set the timer).

CHILI DOGS　　　　　　　12 dogs

This dough is easy to handle.

Dough:
1. In a large bowl gently stir:
   - **1 tablespoon yeast**
   - **1/4 cup warm water**
   - **1 teaspoon honey**
2. When yeast is dissolved, add:
   - **3/4 cup warm water**
   - **2 tablespoons oil**
   - **2 cups flour**
3. Beat this 100 times, let it rest 10 minutes.
4. Beat in:
   - **1 cup flour**
   - **1/2 teaspoon salt**

   If dough is sticky, add a little more flour.
5. Pat a little oil on top of the dough, cover the bowl and let rise in a warm place for one hour. (Set the timer.)

Chili Filling:
1. Measure into a 2-quart bowl:
   - **1 cup TVP** (see page 7)
   - **7/8 cup boiling water**
2. Heat in a heavy two-quart saucepan :
   - **2 tablespoons oil**
3. Fry these for 5 minutes over medium heat, then add the TVP and cook 5 minutes more.
4. Add to the pan:
   - **1 (6-oz.) can tomato paste**
   - **1 can water**
   - **1 teaspoon chili powder**
   - **1 teaspoon cumin**
   - **1/2 teaspoon garlic powder**
   - **1/2 teaspoon oregano**
   - **1/2 teaspoon salt**
5. Cook and stir this mixture for 10 minutes.

Assembly:

1. Lightly oil two cookie sheets. With oily fingers, press down the dough and divide into two balls.
2. Sprinkle flour on a board and a rolling pin.
3. Lightly roll out one ball of dough into a rectangle about 12 inches long.
4. Spread half of the filling mixture on the dough, then roll it the long way. Slice into 6 pieces and put each slice on the baking sheet. Oil the tops.
5. Repeat with remaining dough and filling.
6. Heat oven to 350°. Meanwhile let dogs rise for 10 or I5 minutes on the baking sheet.
7. Bake for 25 to 30 minutes until lightly browned (set the timer).

"PIGS " IN A BLANKET   makes 10

1. Make the dough for **Chili Dogs** and let it rise.
2. Open and drain:
   1 can vegie-dogs or links (10)
3. Roll half the dough out into a rectangle about 8" x I2". Cut into five strips the short way. Wrap a strip of dough around each link, starting at one end of the link and making a spiral wrap.
4. Oil a cookie sheet and place the dough-wrapped bundles on it; then roll out the other rectangle, cut 5 more strips and roll up" pigs".
5. Heat oven to 350°. Meanwhile, let them rise for 10 to 15 minutes, then bake for 25 to 30 minutes (set the timer), until lightly browned on top.

☆BROWN RICE   about 3 cups

We use brown rice in our classes because it's more nutritious. Serving beans and rice in the same meal gives you complete proteins and lots of vitamins and minerals. If you use white rice, it will take less water and a shorter cooking time.

1. Wash well, then drain in a strainer:
   1 cup brown rice
2. Put it in a saucepan with a tight-fitting lid. Add:
   2 1/2 cups water
3. Bring to a boil, then reduce heat to simmer. Cover and cook 40 to 45 minutes (set the timer), remove from heat and taste a grain to check tenderness.

☆RICE WITH HERBS   6 servings

1. Heat in a heavy 2-quart pan over medium heat:
   3 tablespoons vegetable oil
   1 onion, chopped
   1 cup raw brown rice, washed
2. Fry the onions and rice for about l0 minutes, stirring.
3. Add to the pan:
   2 1/2 cups water
   1 teaspoon salt
   1/2 teaspoon basil
   1/2 teaspoon oregano
   1/2 teaspoon garlic powder
   1/4 teaspoon black pepper
4. Bring to a boil over high heat, then reduce heat to low, cover the pan and cook 40 to 45 minutes, until the liquid is absorbed. Turn off heat and let it sit on burner for 10 minutes, covered.

☆MEXICALI RICE   6 servings

1. Heat the oven to 350°. Oil a 3-quart baking dish.
2. Combine in a large bowl:
    4 cups cooked brown rice (I cup raw)
    2 cups sour cream
    **1 4-ounce can green chilis, drained,
        seeds removed, chopped**
    2 cups grated jack cheese
3. Put the rice mixture into the oiled casserole.
    Sprinkle the top with:
    paprika
4. Place in a hot oven and bake for 30 minutes (set
    the timer).

CHINESE FRIED RICE   6 servings

1. Have ready:
    4 cups cooked Brown Rice
    1 pound tofu, in small pieces
    2 onions, sliced thinly
    2 carrots, cut in thin short sticks
    2 stalks celery, sliced thinly
2. Heat in a large skillet or wok:
    1/4 cup oil
    Stir in the tofu and vegetables for about 10
    minutes over medium high heat.
3. Sprinkle on:
    1/4 cup soy sauce
4. Break up the cooked rice with a fork and stir it in.
5. You may add:
    **1 can sliced water chestnuts, drained
    chopped green onions (as garnish)**

CHINESE EGG ROLLS   makes 25

These are baked in the oven, not deep fried, and though we make them in quantity, they disappear fast! The wrappers or "skins" can be found in the fresh vegetable section of most supermarkets.

Have ready:
        1 package Egg Roll Skins (25 wrappers)

Have a damp towel handy when you open the package, keep towel on them so skins don't dry out.

        1 pound tofu, drained, crumbled

(Frozen tofu works best for these. Defrost tofu and press out excess liquid. If using fresh tofu, drain it well so filling isn't too wet.)

Filling:
1. MIx with the tofu:
        2 carrots, grated
        2 tablespoons soy sauce
        1/2 teaspoon garlic powder
        1/2 teaspoon powdered ginger
        1 teaspoon vinegar
2. Heat a large frying pan and add:
        2 tablespoons oil
        1 1/2 cups shredded napa or savoy cabbage
        1/2 cup celery, thinly sliced
        1 onion, chopped small
3. Fry the vegetables for about 10 minutes, then add:
        2 tablespoons soy sauce
        2 cups fresh bean sprouts
4. Cook a few minutes more, stirring, then add the vegetables to the tofu mixture and mix well.

Assembly:

1. Oil two cookie sheets lightly.
2. Mix in a cup to make a "paste" for sealing:
   ### 2 tablespoons flour
   ### 2 tablespoons water
3. Place a wrapper in front of you like a diamond and put about 1/3 cup of filling in the center. Fold over the left side, then the right side, then the top and bottom. Seal the last corner with a little dab of the paste. Set the roll on the oiled cookie sheet, and lightly oil the top, using a small brush.
4. Continue filling the wrappers until all are used up. (Any leftover filling is good to eat as is.)
5. Heat the oven to 400°.
6. Bake the rolls for 10 minutes, (set timer) then remove tray from oven and turn the rolls over. Return to oven and bake10 minutes more, until light brown. While rolls bake, make sauce.

Dipping Sauce:

Mix in a small bowl:
1/4 cup soy sauce
2 tablespoons vinegar
1/2 minced garlic clove

Vivian prepares
Chinese Egg Rolls.

TOFU POT PIE   6 to 8 servings

Vegetables in a yummy gravy under a pastry crust, baked to a golden brown, makes a wonderful dinner. Thaw trozen tofu before you start. Or use fresh tofu.

Filling:

1. Prepare:
   3 medium potatoes, peeled, cut up
   3 carrots, peeled and sliced
2. Heat to boiling:
   4 cups water
   Add potatoes, cover and cook 10 minutes. (Set the timer).
3. Add sliced carrots to the potato pan. Cook until potatoes are fork-tender. Drain, <u>saving the liquid</u> to use in the gravy, and set aside.

Gravy

1. Heat a heavy 4-quart kettle and add:
   1/4 cup oil
   1 large onion, chopped
   Cook over low heat until soft.
2. Prepare and cook a few minutes:
   1/2 cup celery, sliced
3. Press liquid from:
   1 pound defrosted tofu
   and cut or tear it into bite-sized pieces.
4. Sprinkle the tofu with:
   2 tablespoons soy sauce
5. Mix in well. Add to the pan and stir in:
   1/3 cup flour
6. Measure the potato liquid into a one-quart measure and add enough water to make 4 cups. Pour into the pan and stir well.

7. Add as you cook and stir the gravy:
   2 teaspoons powdered vegetable bouillion
   1/2 teaspoon garlic powder
   1/2 teaspoon thyme
   1/2 teaspoon oregano
   1/4 teaspoon black pepper
8. Cook the gravy 10 minutes, then add the potatoes and carrots. Taste the gravy for seasoning.
9. Pour the filling into a 2-quart round baking dish. The dish should be 9 or 10 inches wide.

Pastry Crust and Assembly:
1. Preheat the oven to 400°.
2. Using a pastry blender, mix until it looks like crumbs:
   1 1/2 cups flour
   3/4 stick margarine or butter
   1/2 teaspoon salt
3. Work in with a fork, to make a ball of dough:
   3 tablespoons ice water
4. On a lightly floured surface, pat and roll the dough to a circle one inch bigger all around than the top of your baking dish. Carefully fold the pastry in half and then again, so you can lift the pastry up and lay it on top of the pie filling. Unfold it to cover the pie.Turn the edges under neatly, then go around the rim of the crust with the tines of a fork, pressing the edges down to seal.
5. Make six 2-inch slashes in the crust with a knife, to let steam escape.
6. Set the pie on a baking sheet, as it may bubble over. Bake about 30 minutes, until the top is lightly browned.

☆NOODLE CASSEROLE   8 servings

1. Put in a large kettle:
   3 quarts water
   1 teaspoon salt.
   Bring the water to a boil over high heat.
2. When it is boiling, put in
   1 pound medium flat noodles
3. Boil these, stirring a few times with a big wooden spoon, about 8 minutes (set the timer). Take one out and taste it to be sure it is cooked. Pour the noodles into a colander to drain. Cover with a towel so they don't dry out.
4. While noodles cook, put into a large bowl:
   1 stick margarine or butter
   1 teaspoon garlic powder
   4 green onions, chopped
   1/4 cup parsley, chopped small
   1 pound tofu, crumbled
   (2 cups of cottage cheese can be used instead of tofu.)
5. Heat the oven to 350°. Oil a 3-quart casserole.
6. Mix the cooked noodles into the bowl with the melted   margarine or butter, stir well, then stir in:
   1/3 cup parmesan cheese
   1/2 cup sour cream
   1/4 teaspoon black pepper
7. When noodles and sauce are well mixed, put them in the oiled casserole. Cover with foil. Bake for 25 minutes. (Set the timer.)

☆MACARONI AND CHEESE   6 servings

The kids think this made-from-scratch dish beats the packaged kind.

1. Heat in a large kettle:
   3 quarts water
2. When the water is boiling, put in:
   1 teaspoon salt
   2 cups elbow macaroni
3. Cook 8 to10 minutes, stirring a few times with a big wooden spoon. Taste a piece to see if it is tender.
4. Drain macaroni in a colander.
5. Combine in a large bowl:
   2 cups sour cream or plain yogurt
   2 cups grated Jack cheese
   and add the drained macaroni.
6. Heat the oven to 350°. Oil a 2-quart casserole.
7. Put the macaroni mixture into the dish.
8. Sprinkle on top:
   1 cup bread or cracker crumbs
9. Dot the top with bits of:
   margarine or butter
10. Put casserole in the oven, bake for 30 minutes. (Set the timer.)

Note: To make bread crumbs, tear up bread (stale bread is fine) and whiz a slice or two at a time in the blender. Or break crackers into the blender. Pour crumbs into a measuring cup or jar and do several times. Keep extra crumbs in a closed container in the refrigerator.

☆LASAGNE 6 servings

Kids are pleased to find that this favorite dish is not hard to make.

1. Bring to a boil over high heat in a large kettle:
    3 quarts water
    1 teaspoon salt
2. Carefully put into the boiling water:
    1/2 pound lasagne noodles
    Stir several times to prevent sticking; boil until tender, drain in colander and rinse in cool water.
3. Have ready:
    4 cups pasta sauce (page 61 or a 32 ounce jar)
    15 ounces ricotta cheese (or 1 pound tofu, well-drained and crumbled)
    1/2 pound mozzarella cheese, grated
4. Heat the oven to 325°.
5. Put a little of the sauce in the bottom of a 9" x 13" pan that is at least 2" deep.
6. Make a layer on the sauce of half the noodles.
7. Dot the noodles with spoonfuls of the ricotta or tofu.
8. Sprinkle on half the mozzarella cheese.
9. Spread with half the remaining sauce.
10. Make another layer of noodles, then the rest of the ricotta, then the rest of the sauce and top with the last of the cheese.
11. Bake in the hot oven for 45 minutes. Cool for 5 minutes before serving.

☆ITALIAN PASTA SAUCE   4 cups

This is enough sauce for one pound of spaghetti cooked according to instructions on the pasta box. It is good over shells or spinach noodles , too.

1. Cook in a heavy 2-quart pan over low heat:
   1/4 cup oil
   1 large onion
   until the onion is soft.
2. Stir in:
   1 (17-ounce) can tomato puree
   1 teaspoon oregano
   2 teaspoons basil
   1 teaspoon garlic powder
4. Mix in a bowl, then add:
   2 teaspoons powdered vegetable bouillon
   2 cups hot water
5. Cook over low heat 20 to 30 minutes, stirring occasionally, while the pasta cooks.
6. Serve the sauce on the cooked, drained pasta and pass a dish of:
   grated parmesan cheese

☆MUSHROOM SAUCE

1. Wash, dry on paper towels and chop:
   8 ounces fresh mushrooms
2. Heat in a large skillet over medium heat:
   2 tablespoons butter or margarine
3. Stir and fry the mushrooms until lightly browned, then add with their liquid to the pasta sauce.

STUFFED SHELLS   6 servings

If you have fresh basil or oregano, use twice as much. Shells are terrific with fresh herbs in the filling.

Tomato Sauce:
1. Heat a heavy 2-quart pan and cook on low heat for 10 minutes:
   - **2 tablespoons olive oil**
   - **1 onion, chopped**
2. Add to the pan:
   - **1 6-ounce can tomato paste**
   - **2 cans water**
   - **1/2 teaspoon salt**
   - **1/2 teaspoon dried basil**
   - **1/2 teaspoon dried oregano**
   - **1/2 teaspoon garlic powder**
3. Cook the sauce for about 20 minutes, stirring a few times.

Shells:
1. Bring to a boil in a large kettle:
   - **3 quarts water**
2. Add (while handling gently):
   - **18 large shells**

   Boil about 15 minutes, until shells are tender. Stir them several times with a big wooden spoon to be sure they don't stick together.
3. Drain shells in a colander, then put back in pan. Put cold water over shells in pan so they don't dry out. Handle shells gently so they don't break while you stuff them.

Filling for Shells:
Mix together in a bowl:

1 pound fresh tofu, crumbled
1/4 cup oil
1 teaspoon oregano
2 tablespoons chopped parsley
1 teaspoon basil
1/2 teaspoon garlic powder
1/2 teaspoon salt

Assembly:
1. Heat the oven to 350°. Oil a 9" x 13" pan.
2. Put one cup of sauce in the bottom on the pan.
3. Stuff the shells with filling and place in the pan. Spoon remaining sauce over shells.
4. Sprinkle the top with:
1/2 cup parmesan cheese
5. Bake for 30 minutes.

☆WORLD'S FAIR SPECIALS   6 servings

1. Have ready:
1 (12-ounce) bag corn chips
2 (16-ounce) cans chili beans
1 onion, chopped
2 tomatoes, chopped
1 cup grated jack cheese
2 cups chopped lettuce
1 cup sour cream, in a dish
1 (6-ounce) jar taco sauce, in a dish
2. Heat the beans in a small saucepan on medium heat. Arrange toppings in bowls.
3. Put a handful of chips on each plate. Top with a big spoonful of beans. Let everyone help themselves to the toppings.

☆ EASY "SAUSAGE" BALLS — 48 balls

This is one of the recipes that the kids wanted to make again and again.

1. Steam in the steamer for 15 minutes:

   8 ounces tempeh (see page 6)

   (Note: If tempeh is frozen, let it defrost completely before steaming.) Let cool after steaming.

2. In a large bowl, sift together:

   3 cups flour
   4 teaspoons baking powder
   1 teaspoon salt

3. Using a pastry blender, cut in until it looks like coarse crumbs:

   1 stick   margarine or butter

4. Grate the tempeh, using large holes of the grater, and add it to the flour mixture.

5. Sprinkle in:

   1 teaspoon thyme
   1 teaspoon oregano
   1 teaspoon sage
   1/3 cup parmesan cheese

   Mix flour, tempeh and seasonings together.

6. Stir in:

   1/2 cup milk

7. Preheat the oven to 375°. Lightly oil 2 cookie sheets.

8. With oily fingers, shape pieces of dough into balls the size of a walnut. Mixture will make 48 balls. Place them on the oiled cookie sheets.

9. Bake for 25 minutes in the hot oven, until lightly browned. (Set the timer.) Remove from oven, serve warm as a snack, or with **Golden Gravy** (page 65) as a main dish.

☆GOLDEN GRAVY   2 cups
This is delicious served on rice or biscuits.

1. Put a 6-cup heavy-bottomed sauce pan on the stove over medium low heat.
2. Put into the pan:
   1/3 cup flour
3. Let the flour toast for about 10 minutes, stirring it a few times.
4. Add:
   1/3 cup good tasting nutritional yeast (see Ingredients, page 7)
   Stir and toast the flour and yeast 5 minutes more.
5. Add:
   1/2 stick   margarine or butter
6. Stir the melted margarine or butter and flour together, using a whisk.
7. Stir together in a small pan:
   2 cups hot water
   2 teaspoons powdered vegetable bouillon
9. Slowly whisk the liquid into the flour mix, keep whisking to keep the gravy smooth. Cook a few minutes, as it thickens and bubbles.
10. Whisk in:
   2 tablespoons soy sauce <u>or</u>
   add a little salt for seasoning. Taste gravy.
   Serve over rice, potatoes, biscuits or **Sausage Balls** (page 64).

KNISHES　　　　　　16 knishes

Dough and the filling both use mashed potatoes.
Or try a filling of kasha (buckwheat groats).

Dough

1. Peel and cut into quarters:
   - **4 big potatoes**

   Cover with water in saucepan and boil until soft.
2. Drain potatoes, put back into pan and mash, with:
   - **1/4 stick　margarine or butter**
   - **1/4 cup milk**
   - **1 teaspoon salt**
3. Stir in a large bowl:
   - **3 cups flour**
   - **2 teaspoons baking powder**
   - **1 tablespoon oil**
   - **1 cup mashed potatoes**
   - **1/2 cup cold water**

   Reserve remaining potatoes for filling. Use your hands to knead the dough smooth. Cover the bowl and let dough rest 30 minutes while you mix the filling.

Filling:

1. Heat in a heavy pan:
   - **2 tablespoons oil**
   - **1 big onion, chopped**

   Fry the onion until tender.
2. Put onion with reserved mashed potatoes and:
   - **1 cup crumbled tofu, or**
   - **1 cup cottage cheese, drained**
   - **1/2 teaspoon garlic powder**
   - **1/2 teapoon thyme**
   - **1/4 teaspoon pepper**
   - **1 cup grated cheese**
   - **1/4 cup chopped parsley**

Assembly:

1. Heat oven to 375°. Oil a baking sheet.
2. Separate dough into 4 balls. On a lightly floured board, roll out a ball into a square, about 1/3 inch thick. Cut into 4 smaller squares.
3. Put 2 to 3 tablespoons of filling in the center of a square, and fold the dough over the filling. Repeat for all the dough.
4. Place knishes on oiled pan. Bake 25 minutes, until golden (set the timer).

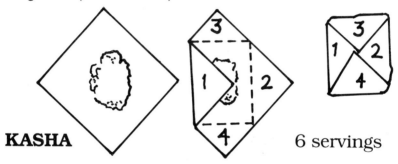

KASHA

6 servings

1. Mix with a fork in a small bowl:
   1 cup kasha (roasted buckwheat groats)
   1 egg
2. Heat in a large pan:
   2 tablespoons margarine or butter
   Add kasha and cook, stirring, until it is light brown and crumbly.
3. Heat to boiling in another pan:
   2 cups water
4. Carefully add water to kasha, standing back to avoid the steam. Stir well, cover the pan, and cook over low heat about 15 minutes.
5. Meanwhile, fry in a heavy skillet on medium heat:
   2 tablespoons oil
   1 large onion, chopped
6. Fluff kasha with a fork and stir in the fried onions. When kasha is cooked, it can be mixed with cooked bow-tie pasta as a main dish, or used as a filling for knishes .

☆**BOOFERS** 6 servings

You can use instant mashed potatoes in these , but then reduce the water added to potato flakes by one third so they aren't too soft to shape into patties.

1. Scrub well and cook in enough water to cover:
   6 potatoes, cut in half
2. Cook 30 minutes, or until fork-tender. While potatoes are cooking, fry over low heat:
   I small onion, chopped
   I tablepoon margarine or butter
3. Drain the potatoes in a colander. Put in a large bowl and mash, adding:
   1/2 stick margarine or butter
   1 teaspoon salt
   the fried onions
4. Prepare and add:
   1 pound tofu, drained and crumbled
   1/4 cup chopped parsley
5. Shape into 12 patties about one-half inch thick as soon as the mixture is cool enough to handle.
6. Heat a pancake griddle or heavy skillet on medium high and oil the surface.
7. Fry the Boofers until nicely browned on the bottom, then carefuly turn over and brown the other side, keeping griddle oiled so they don't stick.

☆NACHO PIE   6 servings

1. Heat oven to 350°.
2. Heat in a 2-quart pan:
     2 16-ounce cans pinto beans (<u>or</u> 4 cups homecooked, with a little of the cooking liquid)
3. When beans are hot, remove from stove and add:
     1 teaspoon chili powder
     1 teaspoon cumin powder
     1 teaspoon garlic powder
     1 teaspoon oregano
     1/4 teaspoon black pepper
4. Mash the beans well. Taste for seasoning. Put bean pan back on the stove and cook over low heat, stirring so they don't stick, until most of the liquid has cooked away. Taste for seasonings.
5. Oil a 9-inch pie pan.
6. Spread beans in the pan.
7. Stick into the beans:
     30 tortilla chips
8. Sprinkle on top:
     1 cup grated cheese
9. Bake 15 minutes.

Sam arranges tortilla chips to top a Nacho Pie.

*Sam and Gretchen fix vegetables
for a Tossed Green Salad.*

SALADS &DRESSINGS

☆Tossed Green Salad • 72

☆Herb Dressing • 72

Macaroni Salad • 73

☆Tofu Salad • 74

☆Cucumber Salad • 74

☆Potato Salad • 75

☆Coleslaw • 76

☆Slaw with Honey Dressing • 76

☆Pineapple Cabbage Salad • 77

Tempuna Salad • 77

☆Summer Mint Salad • 78

☆Pineapple Cheese Salad • 79

☆French Dressing • 79

☆Thousand Island Dressing • 79

☆Carrot Raisin Salad • 80

Waldorf Salad • 80

☆Summer Fruit Salad • 81

Creamy Fruit Salad Dressing • 81

☆Ambrosia • 81

Easy recipes are marked with a ☆

☆TOSSED GREEN SALAD   6 servings

1. Wash and drain in a colander:

   2 quarts fresh salad greens (lettuce, romaine, spinach)

   Then gently pat dry on a clean towel.

2. Tear greens into a salad bowl. Add fresh vegetables, such as:

   tomatoes, cut up
   cucumbers, sliced
   carrots, grated
   onions or avocados, sliced
   red or green pepper strips
   fresh raw mushrooms, rinsed, dried

3. Using a big spoon and fork, toss the salad with enough dressing to lightly coat the greens, two or three tablespoons. Don't use too much.

4. Nice toppers on a mixed salad are:

   bacon bits
   croutons (small cubes of toast)
   grated parmesan or other cheese

☆HERB DRESSING   3/4 cup

1. In a small jar with a tight lid, shake up:

   1/4 cup vinegar
   1/2 teaspoon salt
   1/4 teaspoon dry mustard
   1/4 teaspoon pepper
   1/2 cup vegetable or olive oil

2. Add some herbs for flavor:

   1 teaspoon dill weed, <u>or</u>
   1 teaspoon basil, <u>or</u>
   1 teaspoon oregano, <u>or</u>
   1 teaspoon any herb or combination

   Use your creativity. Use fresh herbs if you have them, then use twice as much. Remaining dressing will keep for days in a covered jar.

MACARONI SALAD   8 servings

1. Heat in a large kettle until boiling:
   3 quarts water
2. Add:
   2 cups elbow macaroni
   and boil 8 to 10 minutes. Stir a few times with a wooden spoon so it doesn't stick to the bottom of the pan.   Lift out a piece to taste to make sure it is tender. Drain the pasta in a colander.
3. Mix in a large serving bowl:
   2 tablespoons oil
   2 tablespoons vinegar
4. Add the drained pasta and stir with a big spoon. Cover the bowl and chill the macaroni.
5. Prepare:
   3 green onions, chopped
   1 cup celery, chopped small
   2 carrots, grated
6. Mix the macaroni with the vegetables and add:
   3 tablespoons mayonnaise
   3 tablespoons sour cream
   Or use all mayonnaise, enough to moisten.
   Add:
   a few dashes of pepper.
   Taste and add a little salt if needed. Chill the salad until serving time.

Other kinds of pasta can be used, try small shells or spirals (rotelle).   Follow directions on package for cooking the pasta.

☆TOFU SALAD   4 servings

1. Drain in a colander:
       1 pound fresh tofu
2. Prepare these vegetables:
       2 green onions, sliced thinly
       2 stalks celery, chopped
       1 medium carrot, grated
3. Using the large holes of the grater, grate the tofu. Or crumble it into a bowl.
4. Mix together the tofu and vegetables. Stir in:
       1/4 cup of mayonnaise
   You may want to add some:
       fresh herbs, chopped <u>or</u>
       pickle relish
5. Taste and add as needed:
       salt and pepper
   Serve the salad on lettuce leaves or use as a filling for sandwiches.

☆CUCUMBER SALAD   6 servings

This mixture makes good sandwiches. Try it on rye or French bread.

1. Slice thinly into a medium bowl:
       2 medium cucumbers
2. Sprinkle with:
       1 teaspoon salt
   Cover bowl and chill 30 minutes (set the timer).
3. Rinse and drain cucumbers, pressing out excess liquid.
4. Mix in:
       1/2 cup sour cream
       2 teaspoons dill weed
   Chill for 30 minutes or more to blend flavors.
5. Stir well before serving.

☆POTATO SALAD   6 servings

1. Heat in a big kettle on medium-high heat:
   2 quarts water
2. Meanwhile, scrub well or peel, then cut in quarters:
   6 potatoes
   Put in the water and cook 20 to30 minutes or until they are fork-tender, (set the timer).
3. Drain potatoes in a colander, put into a bowl, cover, and cool before slicing.
4. Meanwhile, prepare:
   1 onion, chopped small
   1/2 cup celery, sliced thin
   1/4 cup parsley, chopped small
5. Cut the potatoes into smaller pieces, mix with the vegetables and add:
   1/2 cup mayonnaise
   or more, enough to moisten. Taste and add:
   a little salt and pepper
   Some like to add:
   1 tablespoon wet mustard, or
   1 tablespoon pickle juice
6. Chill the salad. Before serving, decorate the top with one or more of these:
   wedges of tomato
   sliced radishes
   slices of pickle
   wedges of hard-boiled eggs
   sprigs of parsley

☆COLESLAW   6 servings

1. Shred, slice thin or chop up:
        3 cups cabbage
    Don't use the tough outer leaves.
2. Prepare:
            2 carrots, grated
            3 green onions, sliced, <u>or</u>
            1 medium onion, chopped small
3.   Mix together then stir in about:
            1/2 cup mayonnaise
    Use more or less, as you like it. Taste and add:
            a little salt and pepper
    Chill well before serving.

☆SLAW WITH HONEY DRESSING

1. Prepare through step #2:
            Coleslaw
2. Shake together in a jar:
            1/4 cup vinegar
            2   tablespoons honey
            1/2   teaspoon salt
            1/8   teaspoon pepper
            1 /2 teaspoon celery seed
            1/3   cup vegetable oil
3. Mix well with the vegetables. Chill the salad.

☆PINEAPPLE CABBAGE SALAD   serves 8

1. Drain:
   1 large can pineapple chunks
   (You can drink the juice.)
2. Chop or shred:
   3 cups cabbage
   Mix the cabbage and pineapple.
3. Mix with a fork in a small bowl:
   1/2 cup plain yogurt
   2 tablespoons mayonnaise
4. Stir this dressing into the salad. Taste and add salt if needed.

TEMPUNA SALAD   6 servings
This makes a delicious sandwich filling.

1. Put steamer basket in a saucepan with a tightly fitting lid. Add water almost to the bottom of the basket. Heat to a simmer. Put in basket:
   8 ounces tempeh (defrosted, if frozen)
   Steam in tightly covered pan for 15 minutes. Remove from pan and cool.
2. Meanwhile, chop up:
   1 small onion
   2 stalks of celery
   2 tablespoons parsley
   1/4 cup pickles
3. Grate the tempeh, using large holes on the grater.
4. Mix together tempeh and vegetables with enough mayonnaise to moisten. Taste the salad and add for seasoning:
   salt and pepper
   Chill. Serve on lettuce or in sandwiches.

☆SUMMER MINT SALAD   6 servings

Wonderful served in pita bread pockets!

1. Put into a pint jar:
   - **2   tablespoons olive oil**
   - **2   tablespoons vegetable oil**
   - **2   tablespoons lemon juice**
   - **1/2 teaspoon salt**
   - **1/4 cup mint leaves, chopped after measuring**

   Nice additions to the dressing are:
   - **1/4 cup raisins <u>or</u> currants, plumped**

   (To plump, measure them into a cup, cover with hot water, let sit 5 minutes, then drain in a strainer.)
   - **1/4 cup toasted sesame seeds**

   (To toast sesame seeds, put in a dry frying pan over low heat for about 10 minutes, shaking the pan a few   times.)
2. Put the cover tightly on the jar and shake dressing.
3. Cut into small cubes and add to the jar:
   - **1/2 pound tofu (1 cup)**

   Shake. Chill until ready to toss the salad.
4. Into a salad bowl, put:
   - **4 cups lettuce, torn up**
   - **2 tomatoes, diced**
   - **1/4 cup onion, chopped**
   - **1 cucumber, diced**
5. Toss the tofu in mint dressing with the lettuce and vegetables. Serve at once.

☆PINEAPPLE CHEESE SALAD   Serves 4

1. Drain:
    1 small can pineapple slices
    (You can drink the juice.)
2. Arrange on plates:
    lettuce leaves
3. Place on the lettuce:
    1 slice pineapple
4. Top with:
    1/4 cup cottage cheese, <u>or</u>
    1/4 cup grated jack cheese
5. Serve with:
    French Dressing

☆FRENCH DRESSING   1/2 cup

1. Put into a small jar:
    1/4 cup vinegar
    1 teaspoon honey
    1/4 teaspoon salt
    1/4 teaspoon paprika
    6 tablespoons vegetable oil
2. Shake well. Keep in covered jar.

☆THOUSAND ISLAND DRESSING   1 cup

1. Mix in a small bowl:
    1 cup mayonnaise
    2 tablespoons chili sauce or ketchup
    1 teaspoon grated onion
    2 tablespoons stuffed olives, finely
    chopped
    and, if you wish, add:
    1 hard boiled egg, chopped small
2. Serve on lettuce, sliced tomatoes, or a salad of mixed
    greens.

☆CARROT-RAISIN SALAD 6 servings

1. Scrub, then grate on the large holes of the grater:
   3 or 4 medium large carrots
   If carrots are soft, put them in ice water for an hour before you grate them.   Don't try to grate the stub ends, just eat them.
2. Mix in a small bowl for dressing:
   1/4 cup mayonnaise
   2 tablespoons yogurt
   1 tablespoon lemon juice
   1 tablespoon honey
3 Mix together:
   the grated carrots
   1/3 cup raisins
   the salad dressing
   Serve in a pretty bowl.

WALDORF SALAD 6 servings

1. Core and cup up:
   4 medium apples
2. Chop fairly small:
   1/2 cup celery
   1/2 cup walnuts
3. Combine in a small bowl:
   1/4 cup mayonnaise
   1 teaspoon honey
   1 tablespoon lemon juice
   1/2 teaspoon celery salt
4. Mix together the apples, celery, walnuts and the dressing, cover and chill until serving time.

☆SUMMER FRUIT SALAD   6 servings

A fruit salad is always the number one favorite.

1. Prepare 5 or 6 cups of fresh fruit, as:

   2 cups watermelon, cut up
   1 cup canteloupe, diced
   1 cup blueberries, washed, drained
   1 cup strawberries, hulled and sliced
   1 cup peaches, peeled, sliced

   You can use varying amounts of any fruits available. Mix fruits together in a bowl, then chill.

2. This can be served on lettuce as a first course, with or without **Creamy Fruit Salad Dressing.**

CREAMY FRUIT SALAD DRESSING

1. Measure into a blender:

   1/2 cup oil
   1/4 cup tofu, crumbled
   1/3 cup honey
   1/2 cup vinegar
   1 tablespoon finely minced onion
   1/2 teaspoon salt
   1/2 teaspoon dry mustard

2. Blend until well mixed and creamy.

☆AMBROSIA   4 servings

1. Put into a medium bowl:

   2 oranges, peeled and cut up
   2 bananas, sliced

2. Cut up and add:

   1 small can pineapple slices with juice

3. Mix well. Spoon into serving dishes. You may sprinkle on top of each:

   1 tablespoon shredded coconut

*Sam cuts up apples for
Apple Bread Pudding*

DESERTS

☆Apple Crisp • 84
☆Caramel Fried Apples • 84
☆Apple Bread Pudding • 85
☆Apple Sauce • 85
☆Gram's Peach Cobbler • 86
☆Baked Bananas • 86
Banana Pudding • 87
☆Chocolate Pudding • 87
☆Graham Cracker Crust • 88
☆Chocolate Pie • 89
☆Tofu Whipped Topping • 89
☆Magic Coconut Pie • 89
Cheesecakes • 90
☆Fudge Cake • 91
☆Chocolate Frosting • 91
Pineapple Upside-Down Cake • 92
Strawberry Shortcake • 93
☆Applesauce Cake • 94
☆Lemon Frosting • 94
Spice Dessert Cake • 95
Lemon Squares • 96
☆Chocolate Mint Squares • 97
☆Brownies • 97
☆Firelighters • 98
☆Chocolate Chip Bars • 99
Oatmeal Cookies • 100
Pecan Rounds • 101
Chocolate Chews • 101
☆Peanut Butter Cookies • 102
☆Chocolate Chip Cookies • 103
Gingerbread Boys & Girls • 104

Easy recipes are marked with a ☆

☆APPLE CRISP   6 servings

1. Oil an 8"x 8" pan. Heat oven to 350°.
2. Slice into the pan:
    6 apples
3. Mix together in a bowl:
    I/2 stick margarine or butter
    I/4 cup honey
    I/2 cup flour
    I cup rolled oats (oatmeal)
4. Spread this crumbly mixture over the apples.
   Sprinkle with:
    cinnamon
5. Bake for 40 to 45 minutes (set the timer), stick a fork
   in the apples to see if they are tender.

☆CARAMEL FRIED APPLES   6 servings

A bowl of these makes a great after-school snack.

1. Cut into quarters, removing the seeds and cores:
    6 apples
2. Put a skillet (big enough to hold all the pieces) over
   medium low heat.
3. Put in the skillet:
    1/2 stick margarine or butter
    1/3 cup honey
4. Cook mixture slowly 5 minutes to make syrup.
5. Lay the apples in the pan (don't burn your fingers).
   Spoon syrup over the top of the apples.
6. Cover the pan, cook on low heat for 10 minutes (set
   the timer) or until apples are tender-crisp.

☆APPLE BREAD PUDDING   6 servings

Serve warm or cold, delicious with ice cream on top.

1. Heat oven to 375°.
2. Oil a one-quart baking dish.
3. Heat in a saucepan:
   1 cup milk
4. Tear up into bite-size cubes:
   6 slices bread
5. Pour hot milk over bread and stir.
6 Peel and cut up:
   3 apples
7. Whisk together in a small bowl:
   1 egg
   1/4 cup honey
   1 teaspoon vanilla
   1/2 teaspoon cinnamon
   1/2 teaspoon nutmeg (optional)
8. Mix together the egg, bread mixture and apples.
9. Pour into the baking dish.
10. Pour boiling water into a bigger pan and set
    pu d ding dish in this.
11. Put both dishes in oven and bake about one hour.
    (Set the timer.)

☆APPLESAUCE   about 2 cups

1. Wash and cut into quarters, removing cores:
   3 big or 4 medium apples
2. Put them in a pan with:
   1/2 cup water
3. Cover and cook slowly until tender, about 15
   minutes (set the timer). Stir now and then.
4. Mash the apples with the potato masher and taste,
   adding a little honey if desired.
5. Sprinkle with:
   cinnamon

☆GRAM'S PEACH COBBLER   6 servings

This batter is good on other fruit, too. Try it with blackberries or strawberries.

1. Coat an 8" x 8" pan with margarine or butter. Heat oven to 350°.
2. Slice into the pan:
   6 fresh peaches, peeled and pitted
3. Sprinkle them with:
   2   tablespoons honey
4. Using whisk, beat until foamy in a medium bowl:
   2   eggs
5. Add to the eggs
   2   tablespoons water
   2   tablespoons honey
   2/3 cup flour
   1   teaspoon baking powder
6. Mix the batter well with the whisk. Pour batter on peaches and bake 30 minutes, until top is lightly browned. Serve warm.

☆BAKED BANANAS   4 servings

1. Heat the oven to 350 °.
2. Spread the bottom of an 8" x 8" baking dish with margarine or butter.
3. Peel and cut in half the long way:
   4   bananas
4. Arrange the banana halves in the dish.
5. Drizzle syrup on each, use a teaspoon to measure:
   8   teaspoons maple syrup for all
6. Put the dish in the oven and bake for 15 minutes (set the timer). Serve warm.

☆BANANA PUDDING   4 servings

Make this in two batches so it will be creamy, then mix the two batches together.

1. Measure into a bowl:
   - **1/2 pound tofu, crumbled**
   - **2 tablespoons vegetable oil**
   - **2 tablespoons orange juice**
   - **2 tablespoons honey**
   - **2 bananas, sliced**
2. Stir these together, then put half in the blender.
3. Turn blender on and off to blend. When the blender is off, use a rubber scraper to push the mix down the sides. Blend until the mixture is creamy.
4. Put pudding into a clean bowl, blend the rest of the mixture until it is creamy, then mix batches together.

☆CHOCOLATE PUDDING   6 servings

1. Measure into a heavy-bottomed pan:
   - **3 tablespoons cornstarch**
   - **3 tablespoons cocoa or carob powder**
   - **3 tablespoons honey**
   - **2 cups milk**
2. Place pan over medium heat and use a whisk to keep stirring the mixture as it cooks. This will prevent lumps and sticking. Cook until it thickens and starts to bubble, whisking. Remove from heat.
3. Stir into the pudding:
   - **I teaspoon vanilla**
4. Pour into serving dishes, cover and cool. Or use as filling for a chocolate pie.

☆GRAHAM CRACKER CRUST   1 crust

1. Lightly coat a pie plate with margarine or butter. Heat the oven to 375°.
2. Place in a plastic bag:
       16   square graham crackers,   crumbled
   Close the top of the bag and roll out the crumbs until they are small, using a rolling pin. Put the crumbs in a small bowl.
3. Mix crumbs with:
       2   tablespoons honey
       1/3   cup melted margarine or butter
4. With the back of a spoon, press crumbs evenly into the bottom of the pan and up the sides.
5. Bake 12 minutes (set the timer). Remove from oven and cool before filling.

Jody makes Graham Cracker Crust.

☆CHOCOLATE PIE   6 servings
1. Make:
   Graham Cracker Crust, page 88
   Chocolate Pudding, page 87
2. Pour pudding into cooled, baked crust. Chill.
3. Top with :
   Whipped Cream or Tofu Topping

TOFU WHIPPED TOPPING   1 cup
1. Combine in a blender or food processor:
   1/2 pound tofu, crumbled
   1/4 cup vegetable oil
   3   tablespoons honey
   1   teaspoon vanilla
   1/4 teaspoon salt
2. Blend until smooth. Pour into bowl, chill.

☆MAGIC COCONUT PIE   8 servings
This pie makes its own crust and topping as it bakes.
1. Heat the oven to 350°. Grease a pie pan with butter or margarine.
2. Measure into a blender:
   2 cups milk
   1/4 cup honey
   1/4 cup melted butter or margarine
   3 eggs
   1/2 cup flour
   1 cup unsweetened coconut
   1 teaspoon vanilla
3. Cover the blender, mix on high speed 10 seconds.
   (You can count to 10 slowly). Pour into the pie pan.
   Bake for 45 minutes.

CHEESECAKE   8 servings

You will need:
  1 Graham Cracker Crust (see page 88)
  Don't pre-bake it for this cheesecake.

1. Heat the oven to 350°.
2. Mix until smooth and creamy in a food processor, or measure into a bowl and then mix in two batches in a blender:
     1 pound tofu, crumbled
     1/3 cup honey
     1/3 cup brown sugar, packed
     1/4 cup vegetable oil
     2 tablespoons lemon juice
3. When mixture is smooth, add:
     2 tablespoons flour
     1 teaspoon vanilla
     1/4 teaspoon salt
4. Process until well mixed. If you have made it in two batches, stir them together. Pour it into the crust. Bake at 350° for 50 minutes (set the timer).

STRAWBERRY CHEESECAKE
1. Wash and slice:
     2 cups fresh strawberries
   Berries can be sweetened with a little honey.
2. Arrange on top of the cooled cheesecake.

CAROB CHIP CHEESECAKE
As soon as it comes out of the oven, dot the top with:
     1/2 cup chocolate or carob chips

☆FUDGE CAKE   15 pieces

1. Heat oven to 350°. Grease a 9" x 13" pan.
2. Sift together into a big bowl:
   2 cups flour
   1 1/2 cups sugar
   1 teaspoon baking soda
   1 teaspoon salt
   1/3 cup cocoa
3. Cut into flour with a pastry blender:
   l stick butter or margarine
4. When the mixture is creamy, stir in:
   1/2 cup hot water
5. Mix well, then stir in:
   1 cup sour cream (store-kind)
   1 teaspoon vanilla
6. Stir the cake batter well, then spoon it evenly into the greased pan. Bake in the preheated oven for about 30 to 35 minutes. Set the timer. Cake is done when it begins to pull away from the sides of the pan. Or you can stick a toothpick in the center and if it comes out clean, cake is done. Let the cake cool completely before you frost it.

☆CHOCOLATE FROSTING

1. Mix in a medium size bowl:
   2 tablespoons butter or margarine
   2 tablespoons milk
2. Beat in, a little at a time:
   2 tablespoons cocoa
   2 cups powdered sugar
3. When frosting is creamy, stir in:
   1 teaspoon vanilla
4. Spread on the cooled cake with a spatula. It is easiest if you drop spoonfuls of the frosting onto the top of the cake evenly spaced, then swirl them together. Cut cake into 15 pieces.

PINEAPPLE
UPSIDE-DOWN CAKE   8 servings

1. Heat the oven to 350°.
2. Melt over low heat in a 10-inch ovenproof skillet or in a 9" x 9" pan:
   1/4 cup margarine or butter
3. Sprinkle in evenly:
   3/4 cup brown sugar
4. Drain and arrange in the pan on the sugar:
   1 17-ounce can pineapple slices
5. Cream together with a big slotted spoon:
   1 stick margarine or butter, softened
   1 cup sugar
   2 eggs, beaten lightly
6. Sift onto a piece of waxed paper:
   2 cups flour
   1 tablespoon baking powder
7. Measure out:
   2/3 cup milk
8. Add half the milk to the egg mixture, then half the flour, then the rest of the milk and then the rest of the flour, stirring each addition in well. Add:
   1 teaspoon vanilla
9. Pour batter over the pineapple. Put in the oven. Bake for 30 to 35 minutes (set the timer). Remove to a board to cool for 5 minutes.
10. Run a knife around the edges to loosen the cake, then place a large plate over the pan. Using pot holders and using both hands, flip the plate and pan upside down so cake comes out with the pineapple on top. Cut into 8 wedges or squares and serve warm.

STRAWBERRY SHORTCAKE   8 servings

1. Wash, remove the hulls from:
   1 quart fresh strawberries
2. Cut them in half, sprinkle with:
   2 tablespoons sugar or honey
3. Heat the oven to 400°.
   Grease well an 8" layer cake pan.
4. Sift into a medium-size bowl:
   2 cups flour
   4 teaspoons baking powder
   1 teaspoon salt
   2 tablespoons sugar
5. Cut in with a pastry blender:
   3/4 stick margarine or butter
6. When mixture is crumbly, stir in:
   3/4 cup milk
7. Push the dough into a ball, then flatten it out   to a circle to fit the greased pan.
8. Bake in the hot oven for 25 minutes.
9. Remove from the oven and cool for 5 minutes. Carefully flip upside down onto one plate then right side up on the serving plate. Use a long bread knife (serrated edges) to make two layers by slicing through the middle crosswise.
10. Carefully lift off the top half to another plate. Spread the warm bottom layer very gently with:
    soft margarine or butter
    and spoon half the strawberries over it. Gently set the top layer on the berries. Top with the rest of the berries. Serve warm with:
    ice cream   or whipped cream

☆APPLESAUCE CAKE   15 servings

1. Grease a 9" x 13" pan. Heat oven to 350°.
2. Cream together with slotted spoon in a big bowl:
   1 stick margarine or butter, softened
   1 cup sugar
   1 egg
3. Sift together onto waxed paper:
   2 1/2 cups flour
   1   teaspoon baking powder
   1   teaspoon baking soda
   1   teaspoon cinnamon
4. Measure into a small bowl:
   1 1/2 cups applesauce
5. Add half the flour to the creamed mixture, stir well.
6. Stir in the applesauce.
7. Beat in the rest of the flour. You may add:
   1/2 cup raisins
   1/2 cup nuts, chopped
8. Spread battter evenly in the greased pan.
9. Put in the oven and bake for 30 to 35 minutes (set the timer). A toothpick stuck in the center will come out clean when cake is done.
10. Remove to a board and cool, then frost.

☆LEMON FROSTING   2 cups

1. Grate on smallest holes of grater:
   1   teaspoon grated lemon rind
2. Using a fork, mix it in a small bowl with:
   2   cups powdered sugar
   2   tablespoons lemon juice
   1   tablespoon water
3. Spread frosting on cake with a spatula.

SPICE DESSERT CAKE   10 servings

This cake bakes its own meringue topping.

1. Heat the oven to 350°. Lightly grease a 9" x 11" pan with butter or margarine.
2. Carefully separate the yolks from the whites of:
   2 eggs
   into two bowls.
3. Sift onto a piece of waxed paper:
   2 cups flour
   1 tablespoon baking powder
   1/2 teaspoon salt
   1/2 teaspoon cinnamon
   1/2 teaspoon nutmeg
4. Cream together with a slotted spoon:
   1 stick margarine or butter
   1 cup brown sugar, packed
5. Beat into the egg yolks:
   1/2 cup water
   1 teaspoon vanilla
   Mix well. Add to the butter-sugar mixture.
6. Stir in the flour and spices.
7. Spoon this batter into the greased pan, using a spatula to spread it evenly.
8. Using an egg beater, beat the 2 egg whites until they form soft peaks. Then beat into the whites, a little at a time:
   3/4 cup white sugar
   1/8 teaspoon cream of tartar
9. Beat meringue well, then spread it on top of the spice layer very carefully.
10. Chop up:
    3/4 cup walnuts or pecans
    Sprinkle nuts on top of the meringue.
11. Bake the cake for 25 to 30 minutes (set the timer). The top should be light gold in color. Serve warm.

LEMON SQUARES   9 squares

1. Heat the oven to 350°.
2. Set out an 8" x 8" pan.
3. Sift into a 2-quart bowl:
   1 cup flour
   1/4 cup powdered sugar
4. Cream in, using a slotted spoon:
   1 stick margarine or butter, softened
5. When this is well mixed, pat it evenly into the bottom of the baking pan.
6. Bake this bottom layer at 350° for 20 minutes (set the timer).
7. Remove pan to a board, but don't turn off the oven.
8. While the crust bakes, mix together with a whisk:
   2 beaten eggs
   1 cup sugar
   1/2 teaspoon baking powder
   2 tablespoons fresh lemon juice
   (This filling will be runny.)
9. Pour mixture into the baked bottom crust.
10. Put the pan back in the hot oven for 20 minutes (set the timer).
11. Remove from the oven, place on a board and cool for 30 minutes. If desired, sift over the top:
    1 tablespoon powdered sugar
    Cut into 9 squares and serve on dessert plates.

☆CHOCOLATE MINT SQUARES   16 squares

1. Heat the oven to 350 °. Grease an 8" x 8" pan.
2. Put on a pie pan:
   1/2 cup almonds
   Roast 10 minutes (set the timer), remove from oven and chop them into small pieces. Leave oven on.
3. Melt in a small pan over low heat:
   1 stick margarine or butter
   2 squares chocolate
4. Break into a bowl:
   2 eggs
5. Beat them with a whisk, then add:
   1 cup sugar
6. Beat well. Stir in the melted chocolate. Then add:

   1/2 cup flour
7. Stir in:
   1/2 teaspoon peppermint extract
   and the chopped almonds.
8. Pour into the greased dish
   and bake at 350° for 25 minutes (set the timer). Cool and cut into 16 squares.

BROWNIES   16 squares

Follow directions for
   Chocolate Mint Squares
   but <u>instead of</u> peppermint extract use:
   1 teaspoon vanilla
   and <u>instead of</u> almonds use:
   1/2 cup walnuts, chopped up
   Do not roast the walnuts.

☆FIRELIGHTERS   18 bars

These got their name because they look like chips of wood for starting a fire, but they are delicious.

1. Heat the oven to 325°.
2. Oil a 9" x 9" pan.
3. Combine in a 2-quart bowl with a pastry blender:

   1   stick margarine or butter, softened
   1   tablespoon light corn syrup
   1/2 cup brown sugar
   1   teaspoon vanilla

4. Mix together in another bowl:

   1 3/4 cups oatmeal
   1/3 cup coconut
   1/2 teaspoon baking powder

5. Mix the oatmeal mixture and the margarine or butter mixture together.
6. Press dough into the greased pan. It will be about a half inch thick.
7. Bake at 325° for 20 to 25 minutes (set the timer). Don't let them get too brown.
8. Remove the pan to a board and cool 5 minutes. Cut into 18 bars while warm.

*Melina uses
a pastry blender.*

☆CHOCOLATE CHIP BARS   18 bars

1. Heat the oven to 350°.
2. Grease a 9" x11" baking pan.
3. Cream together with slotted spoon in a 2-quart bowl:
   1 1/2 sticks margarine or butter, softened
   2/3 cup sugar
4. When mixture is creamy, stir in:
   1 egg
   1/4 cup water
5. Sift together onto a piece of waxed paper:
   2 1/2 cups flour
   1 1/2 teaspoons baking powder
   1/4 teaspoon salt
6. Stir flour mixture into the dough until it is well mixed. The dough will be stiff.
7. Stir in:
   1 teaspoon vanilla
   8 ounces chocolate or carob chips
8. Spread the dough evenly into the greased pan.
9. Bake it in the hot oven for 25 minutes (set the timer) until golden brown on top.
10. Remove to a board and cool, but cut into l8 bars while still warm.

OATMEAL COOKIES   70 cookies

1. Heat the oven to 375°. Grease two cookie sheets. You will need to use the cookie sheets more than once, but after one batch is removed, wipe off the sheet with a paper towel, then grease it again.
2. Mix together in a large bowl, using a slotted spoon:
   - **2 sticks margarine or butter**
   - **1 cup brown sugar, packed**
3. When creamy, add and beat well:
   - **1 egg**
   - **1 tablespoon molasses**
   - **1/4 cup milk**
4. Measure and add to the bowl:
   - **1 1/2 cups flour**
   - **1/2 teaspoon salt**
   - **1/2 teaspoon baking soda**
   - **1 teaspoon cinnamon**
   - **2 cups rolled oats (oatmeal)**
5. Stir the mixture well. Plump raisins by pouring hot water over
   - **1 cup raisins** (in a small bowl)
   Drain the raisins well, then stir in last.
6. Drop the dough by teaspoonful onto a greased cookie sheet, making 20 on one sheet. When one sheet is filled, put it in the preheated oven and set the timer for 12 minutes. While that batch is baking. you can fill another sheet.
7. Lift the hot cookies carefully with a pancake turner and set them on waxed paper to cool. Put another batch in the oven and set the timer again.
8. Continue until all the batter is used. Store cookies in a container with a tight fitting lid.

PECAN ROUNDS   20 cookies

1. Heat oven to 350°. Lightly oil a cookie sheet.
2. Beat together with slotted spoon until creamy:
   1 stick margarine or butter, softened
   1 tablespoon honey
3. Chop up very small:
   1 cup pecans
4. Add to them to the margarine or butter mixture with:
   1 teaspoon vanilla
5. Sift onto waxed paper before measuring:
   1 cup flour
6. Stir the flour into the dough, mixing well. You may use your hands. If dough is sticky, add a little bit more flour.
7. Shape pieces of dough into 24 small balls, place on the cookie sheet and flatten a little.
8. Bake for 15 to 20 minutes (set the timer). Don't brown. Cool cookies on waxed paper.

CHOCOLATE CHEWS   about 30

1. Heat oven to 325°. Lightly oil a cookie sheet.
2. Stir together in a large bowl:
   1 can (I4 oz) sweetened condensed milk
   5 cups cornflakes
   1 cup chocolate or carob chips
3. Drop from a teaspoon onto the cookie sheet, shaping with the spoon. Don't put too many on one pan. You will need to bake several batches, one at a time.
4. Bake 15 minutes (set the timer). Remove at once from the cookie sheet using a pancake turner and a spatula, pushing them together while they are warm if they start to fall apart. They will be crisp when cool. Store in a container with a tight lid.

☆PEANUT BUTTER COOKIES 60 cookies

1. Lightly grease 3 cookie sheets. Heat the oven to 375°. Bake a panful at a time on the middle shelf.
2. Cream with pastry blender until well mixed:
    1 stick margarine or butter (softened)
    1/2 cup brown sugar
    1/2 cup white sugar
3. Beat into the mixture with a big spoon:
    1 egg
    1 cup peanut butter
    1 teaspoon vanilla
    1/2   teaspoon salt
    1/2   teaspoon baking soda
5. Sift onto waxed paper before measuring:
    1 1/2 cups flour
6. Stir flour into the dough, then roll dough into small balls between your hands. Place on cookie sheets.
7. Gently flatten each ball with a fork, making crisscross marks.
8. Bake cookies for 12 to 15 minutes (set the timer). Cookies bake best on the middle rack of the oven. Don't let them get brown. Remove from pans while warm.

☆CHOCOLATE CHIP COOKIES   36 cookies

1. Heat the oven to 375°. Lightly oil 2 cookie sheets.
2. Cream with slotted spoon until well mixed:
   1 stick margarine or butter
   1/2 cup honey
   1 egg
3. Sift together:
   1 1/2 cups flour
   1 1/2 teaspoons baking powder
   1/2 teaspoon salt
4. Stir flour into creamed mixture, beat well. Add:
   1 tablespoon water
   1 cup chocolate or carob chips
   1 teaspoon vanilla
5. Drop by teaspoonful onto cookie sheets. Bake 10 to 12 minutes (set the timer). Don't brown.

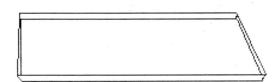

GINGERBREAD BOYS & GIRLS 24 to 30

If you do not have a cutter, make a pattern by folding stiff paper and drawing half a figure on one side, with its middle on the fold. Make it 5 or 6 inches tall. Cut it out. Unfold it and you have a symmetrical figure to use as a pattern for cutting.

1. Cream together in a big bowl:
    1 stick margarine or butter, softened
    1 cup brown or white sugar
2. Beat in:
    1 cup dark molasses
3. Sift together onto a big piece of waxed paper:
    7 cups flour
    2 teaspoons baking soda
    1 teaspoon cinnamon
    2 teaspoons powdered ginger
    1 teaspoon salt
4. Have ready in a measuring cup:
    2/3 cup water
5. Stir one third of the flour and spice mixture into the bowl, then mix in half of the water.   Stir in half of the remaining flour, then the rest of the water. You may have to work in the last of the flour with your hands as the dough will be stiff. Keep the bowl covered with a towel so dough doesn't dry out while you are rolling.
6. Heat the oven to 350°. Lightly grease several cookie sheets.
7. Lightly flour a board and rolling pin.
8. Roll out part of the dough about 1/3 inch thick. Place pattern on dough and with a sharp knife, cut around it. (Or use a shaped cutter.)
9. Using a pancake turner, gently lift the gingerbread figures onto the greased cookie sheet.
10. Repeat until all the dough is used. Press scraps of dough together to roll out again.

11. When one pan is full, put it in the oven and set the timer for 8 minutes.
12. Remove from oven. Lift cookies carefully off the sheet and cool on waxed paper.
13. When all the cookies have been baked, make:
    Gingerbread Icing
14. Decorate the gingerbread kids with a toothpick dipped in icing. Use raisins for eyes if you want.

GINGERBREAD ICING

1. Stir together in a small bowl, using a fork:
    1/2 cup powdered sugar
    1 to 2 teaspoons water
2. If you wish, add a drop or two of:
    food coloring

Erica and Melina make Popcorn Balls.

PARTY FOOD

Good food makes a good party, and you can share your cooking skills with friends. Fix dips ahead of time and a colorful tray of raw vegetables for "dippers". Have crackers and a spread or a plate of fancy sandwiches. Plan on plenty of food for teen-age appetites. Make bars or cookies in the dessert section the day before.

Suggested Party Menu • 108
☆Fancy Sandwiches • 108
☆Stuffed Celery • 108
☆Pink Party Spread • 109
☆Olive-Nut Spread • 109
Green Dip • 110
☆Onion Soup Dip • 110
☆Vegetable Dippers • 110
☆Warm Chili con Queso • 111
☆Cheese Logs • 111
☆Cheese Dollies • 111
Sesame Seed Crackers • 112
☆Mini-Pizzas • 112
☆Popcorn Treats • 113
Popcorn Balls • 113
☆Cracker Jack • 114
☆Chocolate Grahams • 114
☆Peanut Butter Balls • 114
Chocolate Strawberries • 115
☆Stuffed Dates • 115

Easy recipes are marked with a ☆

Suggested Party Menu:
Green Dip with Vegetable "Dippers"
Crackers with Pink Party Spread
Platter of Fancy Sandwiches
Oatmeal Cookies   Brownies
Beverages

☆FANCY SANDWICHES
1. Cut crusts from bread, (save to make crumbs). Use a cookie cutter to make bread rounds. Top with cucumber salad slices (page 74).
2. Make tofu salad sandwiches with two slices of bread and cut each sandwich on the diagonal to make four triangles.
3. Make nut bread (page 19) the day before, slice it thinly and spread with softened cream cheese. Cut each slice in to thirds.
4. OPEN FACE SANDWICHES: Cut slices of bread into rounds or triangles and spread with olive-nut spread (page 109).
6. Spread crackers with pink party spread, top each with a slice of stuffed olive.
7. Keep sandwiches covered and chilled so they don't dry out. Just before serving time, decorate the platter with sprigs of parsley.

☆STUFFED CELERY
Cut celery stalks into two-inch lengths. Fill the hollow with pink party spread or with peanut butter.

☆PINK PARTY SPREAD

1. Mash together with a fork:

    1 8-ounce package cream cheese
    2 tablespoons milk
    1/2 teaspoon paprika
    1/2 teaspoon onion juice

(To get juice, cut an onion in half and scrape flat side.)

Gretchen mashes cream cheese
for Pink Party Spread.

☆OLIVE NUT SPREAD

1. Combine in a small bowl:

    1/2 cup chopped ripe olives
    (or use stuffed green olives)
    1/4 cup chopped walnuts
    2 tablespoons mayonnaise

2. Cut bread slices into rounds or triangles, then spread with the olive mixture. Serve Open-Face.

GREEN DIP   3 1/2 cups

This makes a lot, but you can make it ahead .

1. Thaw and drain well, pressing out excess juice:
   1 (10 oz.) package chopped spinach
2. Put spinach in the blender or processor with:
   1 package dried leek soup mix
3. Blend until well mixed. Pour into a bowl and stir in:
   2 cups sour cream or plain yogurt
   Keep this covered and chilled until serving time.
   It's good with potato chips, as well as raw vegies.

☆ONION SOUP DIP   2 cups

1. Stir together until well mixed:
   1/3 cup dried onion soup mix
   2 cups sour cream
2. Cover bowl and chill 2 hours before serving.

☆VEGETABLE DIPPERS

Fix a pretty platter or bowl with your choice of:
> **carrots, peeled and cut in sticks**
> **celery, trimmed and cut in sticks**
> **green or red pepper, cut in strips**
> **cherry tomatoes, whole**
> **fresh mushrooms, sliced thickly**
> **cucumber, peeled, cut in sticks**
> **zucchini, cut in sticks**
> **broccoli, broken up into flowers**
> **cauliflower, broken up into flowers**
> **radishes, whole, trimmed**

☆WARM CHILI CON QUESO DIP

This is great with corn chips or tortillas.

1. Heat in a small pan:
   1 8-ounce jar Picante or Taco Sauce
   1/2 teaspoon garlic powder
2. When it's warm, stir in to melt:
   1 cup grated jack cheese (4 oz.)

☆CHEESE LOGS   6 logs

1. Have ready:
   12 slices thin-sliced bread
   12 square slices of cheese
   mustard
   margarine or butter, softened
   toothpicks
2. Heat oven to 400°.
3. Trim crusts from bread, spread each slice with mustard, place a slice of cheese on the bread. Pull two opposite corners together and fasten with a toothpick. Spread soft margarine or butter on the outside of each log.
4. Place on a baking sheet and bake for 10 minutes in the hot oven until lightly browned.

☆CHEESE DOLLIES   16

1. Heat oven to 425°. Oil a baking sheet.
2 . Mix with a large spoon:
   1 cup flour
   1 cup grated cheese
   1/2 teaspoon salt
   3/4 cup milk
3. Drop by tablespoon one inch apart on the sheet.
4. Bake only 7 to 9 minutes in the oven (set the timer for 7 minutes). Remove from sheet while warm.

SESAME SEED CRACKERS

1. Combine in a bowl using a pastry blender:
   1   stick margarine or butter
   1 1/2 cups flour
   1/2   teaspoon salt
   1 dash cayenne pepper
2. Have ice water in a cup and add only a spoonful or two -- just enough to moisten so it forms a ball.
3. Heat the oven to 375 °.
4. Lightly oil a cookie sheet.   Roll out the dough between two sheets of waxed paper very thinly. Cut into squares or diamonds. Lift pieces carefully onto the baking sheet. Use a fork to prick top of dough all over.
5. Sprinkle evenly over the top:
   2/3   cup sesame seeds
6. Bake in the hot oven for 12 to 15 minutes, until lightly browned.

☆MINI -PIZZAS   12

1. Have ready:
   6   English muffins, cut in half
   1   onion, thinly sliced
   1   green pepper, thinly sliced
   1/2 cup stuffed olives, sliced
   1 cup (4 oz.) grated cheese
2. Mix together in a small bowl:
   1 (8 oz.) can tomato sauce
   1 teaspoon oregano
   1 teaspoon basil
3. Spread muffins with tomato mixture, then arrange onions, peppers, olives and cheese on top.
4. Heat the broiler. Place muffin halves on a cookie sheet. Put under the broiler on an oven rack about 4 inches from the heat. Broil until cheese bubbles, leaving oven door open. Serve hot.

☆POPCORN TREATS   about 1 quart

How to make popcorn:

1. Heat in a big pot with a good lid over medium high heat:
    1 tablespoon oil
    Drop in a test kernel to see if the oil is hot enough.
2. If the test kernel pops right away, pour in:
    1/4 cup popcorn kernels
    Cover the pan and shake until the popping stops.
3. Pour into a big bowl. For eating, melt:
    2 tablespoons margarine or butter
    and stir into the popped corn.
    Use plain unbuttered popcorn to make balls.
    Or try popcorn mixed with **raisins and peanuts.**

☆CHEESE CORN

Sprinkle the popped corn with:
2 tablespoons parmesan cheese

POPCORN BALLS   15

1. Pop in two batches by directions above:
    1/2 cup corn kernels
2. Combine in a 1-quart pan:
    2 tablespoons margarine or butter
    1 1/2 cups brown sugar, packed
    6 tablespoons water
3. Stir and cook until it boils. Use caution: the syrup will be **very** hot. Boil without stirring until it tests for the soft-ball stage. Test every 2 minutes.
4. To test, have ready:
    1 cup cold water
    Drop a little syrup into the water from a teaspoon, and try to press it into a soft ball. As soon as it will press together, remove pan from stove.
5. Pour syrup over popcorn quickly, mixing with a large spoon, trying to coat every kernel. When it's cool enough to handle, rub a little margarine or butter on your hands and shape hot corn into balls.

☆CRACKER JACK

1. Mix together in a big bowl:
   2 quarts of popped corn
   1 cup roasted peanuts
2. Heat the oven to 350°.
3. Cook in a small pan a few minutes:
   1 stick melted butter or margarine
   1 teaspoon molasses
   1/3 cup honey
4. Pour syrup mix over popcorn, stirring with a big spoon to mix well. Spread mix out on a cookie sheet. Bake for 10 minutes. It will be crispy when cool.

☆CHOCOLATE GRAHAMS

1. Have ready:
   graham crackers
   peanut butter
   chocolate or carob chips
2. Heat the oven to 325°.
3. Spread peanut butter lightly on the crackers and place them on a cookie sheet. Dot the top of each with chocolate or carob chips.
4. Place sheet in the oven and bake about 10 minutes or until the chocolate is melted. Lift out onto serving plates and cool.

☆PEANUT BUTTER BALLS

1. Mix in a small bowl:
   1/2 cup peanut butter
   1/2 cup honey
2. Add and mix in well:
   3/4 cup dry powdered milk
   Roll this mixture into small bite-sized balls.
3. Put on a piece of waxed paper:
   1/2 cup grated coconut
4. Roll the balls in coconut then put on a serving plate.

CHOCOLATE DIPPED STRAWBERRIES　24

The most elegant party dish you could serve your guests,
and you can make them the day before.

1.　Wash, <u>but leave on the green leaves:</u>
　　　24 large strawberries
　　　Dry them on paper towels.
2.　Melt in a small pan set in a pan of hot water:
　　　8 ounces chocolate or carob chips
3.　Line a platter with waxed paper. Carefully hold each berry by its leaves and dip it into the melted chocolate, covering the berry with chocolate on the bottom two-thirds of the berry. This leaves some red showing. Place each dipped berry on the waxed paper. Chill before serving.

☆STUFFED DATES

1.　Packaged, pitted dates need not be washed. Stuff each date with large pieces of pecans or walnuts and press edges together. They can be rolled in coconut or powdered sugar, if desired.

2.　Or try filling with peanut butter, shaped by your fingers, or use cream cheese softened with a little orange juice.

SETTING THE TABLE

An attractive table sets the stage for the food you have prepared. Follow the diagram to set each place neatly. Use a tablecloth or place mats, cloth or paper napkins.

Flowers, a house plant or an arrangement of fresh fruits in a bowl make a pretty centerpiece. Candles add a nice touch. Use protective mats under hot foods and protect a wooden table with coasters under cold beverages.

PLACE SETTING

1. SALAD PLATE	6. KNIFE
2. NAPKIN	7. SOUP SPOON
3. SALAD FORK	8. TEASPOON
4. DINNER FORK	9. BREAD PLATE
5. DINNER PLATE	10. GLASS

Fancy Butter: Slice butter into pats, decorate each with a small piece of fresh parsley. Keep chilled.

INDEX

Alphabet Soup, 36
Ambrosia, 81
Apple Bread Pudding, 85
Apple Crisp, 84
Apple Pancakes, 10
Apple Sauce, 85
Apples, Caramel Fried, 84
Applesauce Cake, 74

Baked Bananas, 86
Baking Powder Biscuits, 12
Banana Pudding, 87
Barley Soup, Pea and , 40
Basic Fancy Roll Dough, 28
Bean Burritos, 46
Bean Soup, Black, 39
Beans from Scratch, 47
Biscuits,
    Baking powder 12
    Drop 14
Black Bean Soup, 39
Blueberry Coffee Cake, 18
Blueberry Muffins, 15
Blueberry Pancakes, 10
Boofers, 68
Bread Pudding, Apple 85
Bread,
    Cuban 24
    Date-Nut 20
    Hot Garlic 24
    Nut Bread 19
    Oatmeal 25
    Orange 19
    Peanut Butter 21
Breadsticks, 27
Brown Rice, 52
Brownies, 97
Buns, Burger 30
Buns, Honey 29
Burritos, 46
    Bean Burritos 46
    Tofu Burritos 47
Butterhorn Rolls, 29

Cabbage Salad, Pineapple 77
Cake,
    Applesauce 74
    Blueberry Coffee 18
    Fudge 91
    Pineapple Upside-Down 92
    Spi ce Dessert 95
Caramel Fried Apples, 84
Carrot Raisin Salad, 80
Casserole, Noodle, 58
Celery, Stuffed, 108
Cheese Biscuits, 14
Cheese Corn, 113
Cheese Logs, 111
Cheesecakes, 90
Chili, 44
Chili & Cornbread Topper, 44
Chili con Queso, 111
Chili Dogs, 50
Chinese Egg Rolls, 54
Chinese Fried Rice, 53
Chocolate Chews,101
Chocolate Chip Bars, 99
Chocolate Chip Cheesecake, 90
Chocolate Chip Cookies, 103
Chocolate Frosting, 91
Chocolate Grahams, 114
Chocolate Mint Squares, 97
Chocolate Pie, 89
Chocolate Pudding, 87
Chocolate Strawberries, 115
Cinnamon Rolls, 13
Cloverleaf Rolls, 28
Cobbler, Peach 85
Coconut Pie, Magic 89
Coffee Cake, Blueberry 18
Coffee Cake, 18
Coleslaw, 76
Cookies,
    Chocolate Chip 103
    Chocolate Graham 114
    Oatmeal 100
    Peanut Butter 102

Corn Chowder, 38
Cornbread in a Skillet, 17
Cracker Jack, 114
Crackers, Sesame Seed, 112
Creamy Sweet-Sour Dressing,81
Croutons, 40
Crust, Graham Cracker, 88
Crust, Pastry, 57
Cuban Bread, 24
Cucumber Salad, 74

Date Muffins, 16
Date Nut Bread, 20
Dates, Stuffed 115
Dip, Green 110
Dip, Onion 110
Dippers, Vegetable, 110
Dressing, Herb 72
Drop Biscuits, 14
Drop Cheese Biscuits, 14

Easy "Sausage" Balls, 64
Easy Enchiladas, 49
Egg Rolls, Chinese 54
Enchilada Casserole, 48

Fancy Roll Dough, Basic 28
Fancy Sandwiches , 108
Firelighters, 98
French Dressing, 79
French Toast, 12
Fried Apples, Caramel 84
Fried Rice, Chinese 53
Frosting, Chocolate 91
Frosting, Lemon 94
Fruit Salad, 81
Fudge Cake, 91

Garlic Bread, 24
Gingerbread Boys & Girls, 104
Gingerbread Icing, 105
Golden Gravy, 65
Green Dip, 110
Green Salad, Tossed 72

Herb Dressing, 72
Honey Buns, 29
Honey Topping, 11

Icing, Gingerbread 105
Italian Pasta Sauce, 61
Italian Rolls, 26

Kasha, 67
Knishes, 66
Kolacky, 31

Lasagne, 60
Lemon Frosting, 94
Lemon Squares, 96
Lentil Soup, 35

Macaroni and Cheese, 59
Magic Coconut Pie, 89
Mexicali Rice, 53
Minestrone, 41
Mini-Pizzas, 112
Mint Salad, Summer 78
Miso Soup with Tofu, 37
Muffins, 15
Mushroom Sauce, 61

Nacho Pie, 69
Noodle Casserole, 58
Nut Bread, 19
Nut Bread, Date 20

Oatmeal Bread, 25
Oatmeal Cookies, 100
Olive-Nut Spread, 109
Onion Dip, 110
Orange Bread, 19

Pancakes, 10
Party Menu, Suggested 108
Party Spread, Pink 109
Pasta Sauce, Italian 61
Pastry, 57
Pea and Barléy Soup, 40
Peach Cobbler, Gram's 86
Peanut Butter Balls, 114
Peanut Butter Bread, 21
Peanut Butter Cookies, 102
Pecan Rounds, 101
Pecan Waffles, 11
Pie, Chocolate 89
Pie, Magic Coconut 89

Pigs in a Blanket, 51
Pineapple Cabbage Salad, 77
Pineapple Cheese Salad, 79
Pineapple Upside-Down Cake, 92
Pink Party Spread, 109
Pizza, 45
Pizzas, Mini 112
Popcorn Balls, 113
Popcorn Treats, 113
Poppy Seed Rolls, 127
Pot Pie, Tofu 56
Potato Salad, 75
Potato Soup, 85
Pudding, Apple Bread 85
Pudding, Banana 87
Pudding, Chocolate 87

Raisin Bran Muffins, 16
Rice and Tomato Soup, 38
Rice,
    cooking from scratch 52
    Chinese Fried 53
    Herb 52
    Mexicali 53
Roll Dough, Basic Fancy 28
Rolls,
    Basic Fancy Dough 28
    Butterhorns 29
    Cinnamon 13
    Cloverleaf 28
    Italian 26
    Poppy Seed 27

Salads, 71-81
Salad Dressing,
    Creamy Sweet-Sour 81
    French 79
    Herb 72
    Thousand Island 79
Sandwiches,
    Fancy 108
Sauce,
    Dipping 54
    Italian Pasta 61
    Mushroom 61

Sesame Seed Crackers, 112
Shells, Stuffed 62
Shortcake, Strawberry 93
Skillet Cornbread, 17
Slaw with Honey Dressing, 76
Soft Burger Buns, 30
Soups, 34-41
Spice Dessert Cake, 95
Spread, Olive-Nut 109
Spread, Pink Party 109
Strawberries,
    Cheesecake 90
    Chocolate Dipped 115
    Shortcake 93
Stuffed Celery, 108
Stuffed Dates, 115
Suggested Party Menu, 108
Sweet-Sour Dressing, 81

Table Setting, 116
Tempuna Salad, 77
Thousand Island Dressing, 79
Tofu Burritos, 47
Tofu Pot Pie, 56
Tofu Salad, 74
Tofu Whipped Topping, 89
Tomato Soup, 38
Topping, Honey 11
Tortillas, 46
Tossed Green Salad, 72

Upside-Down Cake, 92

Vegetable Dippers, 110
Vegetable Soup, 36

Waffles, 11
Waldorf Salad, 80
Whipped Topping, 89
World's Fair Specials, 63

Cooks in the photographs:

Gretchen Bates
Erica Christopherson
Chris Cook
Sam Gaskin
Ben Rohrbach
Melina Sierra
Jody Stevenson
Vivian Traugot

Order these fine books directly from Book Publishing Co.:

Tofu Cookery $11.95
Tofu Quick & Easy 5.95
Murrieta Hot Springs Vegetarian Cookbook 9.95
Kids Can Cook 8.95
Starting Over: Learning to Cook
   with Natural Foods 8.95
The Farm Vegetarian Cookbook 6.95
Vegetarian Cooking for Diabetics 9.95
George Bernard Shaw Vegetarian Cookbook.... 8.95

Please include $1 per book for postage and handling.

Mail your order to:
   Book Publishing Company
   PO Box 99
   Summertown, TN 38483